Tilikum
Luxton's
Pacific
Crossing

Tilikum
Luxton's
Pacific
Crossing

NORMAN LUXTON

Edited by Eleanor Luxton

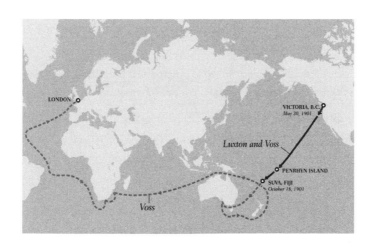

KEY PORTER BOOKS

National Library of Canada Cataloguing in Publication Data

Luxton, Norman Kenny, 1876–1962
      Tilikum: Luxton's Pacific crossing

First published 1971 under title: Tilikum
ISBN: 1-55263-449-3

1. Luxton, Norman Kenny, 1876–1962—Journeys—Oceania. 2. Tilikum (Canoe). 3. Oceania—Description and travel. I. Luxton, Norman Kenny, 1876–1962 Tilikum. II. Title.

G477.L98 2002   919.504   C2002-901147-7

THE CANADA COUNCIL | LE CONSEIL DES ARTS
FOR THE ARTS | DU CANADA
SINCE 1957 | DEPUIS 1957

ONTARIO ARTS COUNCIL
CONSEIL DES ARTS DE L'ONTARIO

The publisher gratefully acknowledges the support of the Canada Council for the Arts and the Ontario Arts Council for its publishing program.

We acknowledge the financial support of the Government of Canada through the Book Publishing Industry Development Program (BPIDP) for our publishing activities.

Key Porter Books Limited
70 The Esplanade
Toronto, Ontario
Canada M5E 1R2

www.keyporter.com

Design: Peter Maher
Electronic formatting: Heidi Palfrey

Printed and bound in Canada

02 03 04 05 06 6 5 4 3 2 1

Acknowledgements

I wish to express my gratitude to Dr. George F. G. Stanley, Professor of Canadian Studies at Mount Allison University, who encouraged, advised and actively assisted me in completing this book, and to Dr. Willard E. Ireland, Director and Archivist of the Provincial Archives of British Columbia, who helped to clarify many obscure points in the text. I am happy to acknowledge with sincere appreciation the assistance of many others including Mr. John A. Bovey, Archivist, Provincial Library and Archives, Winnipeg, Manitoba; Colonel J. W. D. Symons, Director, Maritime Museum of British Columbia; Miss E. Mooney, Librarian, The Press Library, Vancouver, B.C.; Mr. Gerald Brawn, Public Relations Director, *Calgary Herald*; Mrs. S. J. Vale, Winnipeg, Manitoba; Miss Patricia Luxton, Minneapolis, Minnesota. To these obligations, I would add those I owe to the staffs of the Archives of the Canadian Rockies, Banff, Alberta; Glenbow Foundation, Calgary; and the Provincial Archives of British Columbia, Victoria, B.C.; the National Maritime Museum, Greenwich, England; Royal Geographical Society, London, England; The Library, University of Canterbury, Christchurch, New Zealand; University of Otago, Dunedin, New Zealand; Library of Congress, Washington, D.C.

—ELEANOR G. LUXTON

Contents

Foreword to the Second Edition

My initial contact with this great Canadian adventure story was inauspicious. I was twelve years old when the first edition of this book came out, and I remember it well. I had been dragged from our home in Calgary to Aunt Eleanor's book launch. It was a small gathering in the lower level of the Archives of the Canadian Rockies facing the Bow River, in Banff. I wasn't very interested. Aunt Eleanor was a bit like Miss Havisham to me. A formal, dark-haired woman, damaged but not broken by multiple sclerosis, she smoked cigarettes from a long black cigarette holder, behind whose smoke was a piercing gaze. She did not suffer clumsy little boys gladly.

I survived the book launch, but found it formal and boring. What was the big deal about a canoe trip on the Pacific? My mother told me to read the book. She said it was a story to match *Kon Tiki*, Thor Heyerdahl's well-known tale of a papyrus raft sailing trip. Of course I didn't read it. A book about Aunt Eleanor's father, a distant relative who published a small newspaper in Banff, just didn't capture my imagination.

Thirty years later, living in Cambridge, Massachusetts, I found myself looking for a book to take on a canoe trip down the Thelon River in the wilderness of the Northwest Territories and Nunavut. My eyes strayed to *Luxton's Pacific Crossing*. My interest in family had grown considerably since Aunt Eleanor's book launch, as had my understanding of the remarkable Luxtons. So, in the wilds of the Canadian Arctic, I began to read Norman Luxton's account of his canoe voyage with a man named Voss. I couldn't put it down. But I still wondered: was it as significant an event in a global context—this crossing of the Pacific by dugout canoe—as the foreword by George Stanley and introduction by Eleanor Luxton made it out to be?

Sitting around the campfire one night, I happened to mention the *Tilikum*. John Jennings, one of my companions on the trip, exploded: "The *Tilikum* is one of the most famous canoes in the world! Its voyage is clearly the longest canoe voyage in history!" (He pointed out that the *Tilikum* was sailed not paddled.) Jennings ought to know. He is the vice chair of the Canadian Canoe Museum in Peterborough, Ontario, and editor of *The Canoe in Canadian Cultures*. Another companion, Peter Allen, knew of its significance, too. A passionate sailor from Toronto, he knew all about the *Tilikum*'s famous captain, John Claus Voss, who along with Joshua Slocum was one of the legendary mariners of the late nineteenth and early twentieth centuries. But neither man knew much about Norman Luxton—the mate of the *Tilikum*—or knew this book existed.

Norman Luxton was the son of the publisher of the *Winnipeg Free Press*. Born in 1876, he was among the first western Canadians to come from a leisure class who had the time to learn to write well. He also had the financial ability and class inclination to be an adventurer for the sake of the exploration rather than an explorer for commercial purposes. He was a literate young man in an era of great romantic adventurers like Stanley and Livingston in Africa and

Theodore Roosevelt in the tropics and the American west. Norman Luxton caught the bug of his times.

He voyaged on the great inland sea of Lake Winnipeg in a York boat (a twelve-metre open watercraft used in the fur trade). He canoed from British Columbia to Lake Ontario. He moved from the metropolis of Winnipeg to the frontier town of Calgary, where he worked as a young journalist at the *Calgary Herald* for eight years.

But Calgary couldn't hold Norman. He moved on to Vancouver and worked as a journalist there—and it was in a bar in that seaport town that he met Captain John Claus Voss, an accomplished seaman, who bragged that he was a greater sailor than Joshua Slocum. Slocum had achieved great fame by sailing around the world in a tiny yawl, the *Spray*. Voss claimed that he could best Slocum by sailing around the world in an even smaller vessel. On a spring night in 1901, Luxton dared Voss to prove his bravado, laying $5,000 and his life on it. He said he'd give Voss half that amount if he took Luxton along and they crossed all three oceans. Luxton would also write about the voyage and give half of the proceeds to Voss.

With Luxton's money, Voss bought a cedar dugout canoe from a Salish Indian, outfitted it, and the two set off. Ten thousand kilometres and six months later, Luxton was a broken man in a Suva, Fiji, sick bed. He and Voss had crossed the Pacific Ocean together in a dugout canoe, but had nearly killed each other out of mutual hatred along the way.

But I won't spoil the story—a story almost never told from Luxton's point of view. Voss, whose continuing voyage became very famous, published his account in *The Venturesome Voyages of Captain Voss* many years later. This infuriated Luxton, and in 1926, he wrote his own version and gave it to his daughter, Eleanor. Seventy years after the fateful voyage, she published it under the title *Luxton's Pacific Crossing*.

Without Eleanor Luxton, this great adventure story would be lost to Canadians. She was a remarkable person. She became a professional engineer in 1940s—at a time when that sort of thing just wasn't done by women—and got a job designing locomotives for the Canadian Pacific Railway. It's hard to know what she could have accomplished had she lived without the burden of multiple sclerosis. But even this disease did not defeat her. She fought it for almost fifty years, wrote *Banff: Canada's First National Park*, saw to the publishing of *Luxton's Pacific Crossing*, and made provisions for the upkeep of the *Tilikum* in Victoria. It is now permanently displayed on the main floor of the Royal Canadian Maritime Museum of British Columbia, which also republished *The Venturesome Voyages of Captain Voss* in 1976.

Eleanor also left a sizeable estate to create the Eleanor Luxton Historical Foundation. The Foundation preserves the Luxton residences on Beaver Street in Banff for public tours and makes grants to support work on western Canadian history connected to the Banff area. Through the Archives of the Canadian Rockies (operated by The Peter and Catherine Whyte Foundation), the Luxton Foundation has also made Norman Luxton's papers available to researchers. Together with Anna Porter of Key Porter Books, the Luxton Foundation has made possible the re-publication of this epic story of one of the great canoe adventures of all time.

—HARVEY LOCKE
Cambridge, Massachusetts
February, 2002

Foreword

The sea has always held a great fascination for men and boys. It is a fascination as old as ships, and ships in their various forms are almost as old as man. Even those who have been bound to the land and have never pitted their strength and their skill against the elements, feel, deep down inside, at least a momentary sense of freedom when they look over the heaving waters that stretch from the shore on which they stand to far-off horizons. No lake, however large, can evoke quite the same primitive response as does the sea. It is this response that explains the continued popularity of sea stories, stories of men who have sailed the seven seas, who have battled the sea in small boats, who have overcome the sea and gained their victories over the elements.

The appeal of the ship is basically the appeal of the sailing ship. Was not the age of exploration the age of sail, the achievement of men who relied upon wind and water to defeat the water and the wind? With the coming of steam some of the excitement and most of the romance has gone out of sea stories in the great billows of smoke that belched from the smoke-stacks of the new iron ships. But our own day and generation has its men who have carried on the tradition of sail.

One of the most notable Canadian contributions to the saga of the small sailing ship was the voyage of the *Tilikum*. A West Coast Indian war canoe, she sailed from Oak Bay, Vancouver Island, to the estuary of the Thames River in the early years of the present century, not long after the voyage of Joshua Slocum's *Spray*. Two men made up her crew—one, John Voss, a man of uncertain origin, uncertain demise and uncertain veracity; the other, Norman Luxton, a man in search of life and the meaning of life.

The whole project was Luxton's. It was his idea and his boat. Luxton had originally planned to write the story of the *Tilikum*, but his later experiences in Banff, Alberta, and with the Indians of the mountain regions, took precedence in his own mind over his sea adventures, and he did no more than prepare a journal based upon his personal diary, assemble a number of photographs taken during the Pacific crossing, and jot down a few comments on a narration written by his companion.

Fortunately, after considerable urging, his daughter, Eleanor Georgina Luxton of Banff, agreed to edit her father's account for publication. In so doing she has added a new dimension to our knowledge of the *Tilikum* odyssey and to our excitement at discovering a hitherto neglected Canadian contribution to the small-boat saga. The Luxton journal is a straightforward factual account which reveals not only the problems of navigating the waters of the less-than-pacific Pacific in a dugout canoe, but the even greater problems of reconciling two men of strong personalities, locked together in a single cabin, during a journey of 10,000 miles. These two men, John Voss and Norman Luxton, shared storms both natural and human, for weeks on end, until they could do so no longer. By making her father's journal available for all to read, Miss Luxton has placed all lovers of sea stories in her debt.

—GEORGE F. G. STANLEY
Professor of Canadian Studies,
Sackville, New Brunswick

Introduction

NORMAN KENNY LUXTON

The journal tells us little of the man Norman Luxton and it is only from letters to his future wife and some subsequent letters to her that we learn more. The following brief biography will be taken mainly from these.

Dear little girl, you want to know more about me, well there is not much to tell. I was born in Upper Fort Garry, later Winnipeg, November 2, 1876 and I am the second son of William Fisher Luxton and Sarah Jane Edwards Luxton. I was not much for school but one teacher, Agnes Laut, had a very good influence. She later became an historian and writer, and to her I owe my love of books. I suppose I was average in that I played the usual tricks to go fishing or to be with George Grieve, who was a naturalist. From George I came to love all Nature and learned my taxidermy.

I like working in father's newspaper office, you know he started the *Winnipeg Free Press* with John A. Kenny as his partner. Did I tell you my second name is his? When I was about sixteen I joined the Indian Agency at Rat Portage [Kenora] as an apprentice clerk. It was pretty dull except when we went north with the Treaty money. I was put in the centre of an eight-man canoe, with a heavy locked steel cash box hanging from my neck by a strap. The theory was if we upset in the rapids the box would be found with my body. Well it never happened, little girl, because I decided to go West. All my life I had been hearing about the Cariboo gold fields and thought I might be one of the lucky ones. I was not so I went back to Calgary, still in the North West Territories and though I was little past seventeen I felt older.

The *Calgary Herald* seemed a likely place to find work. Both J. J. Young, the owner and proprietor, and Tom Braden, the founder, were there when I went to the office. They told me if I would collect some long over-due bills they would hire me. I found a bill two years old for several hundred dollars issued to Jack Donahue, proprietor of the Empire Hotel. How those fellows laughed when I told them I would collect that one first.

I went into the hotel bar-room and the first man I saw was a character, clean shaven, with a Christie stiff pushed back on his head, cutaway coat with tails, thin-striped light coloured pants, and sharp-toed patent leather shoes—Jack Donahue in person. I introduced myself and invited him to have a drink. We matched drink for drink, talking and eating snacks from the bar until closing time. Then, dear girl, you will hardly believe this, Donahue suddenly pulled a roll of bank notes from his tail coat: "Here is my money, drop in again any time."

So I was with the *Herald* for eight years, as reporter, typesetter or man-ager depending on whether either J.J. or Tom was there. It was a good interlude. Paddy Nolan, you know the criminal lawyer, had his office over the *Herald* and we became friends. If both Braden and Young were away and I had to do the editorial I would dash up to Paddy and in no time we had the leading article ready. When the paper was off the press I'd rejoin Paddy to talk, relax and toss for a drink or a cigar.

I might have stayed, but I was always searching for a missing *something* so I went to Vancouver. There I met Frank Burd [who later became proprietor of the *Vancouver Province*]. We decided to put out a weekly gossip sheet called *Town Topics*. We gathered news, met in a small shop where we had an old hand press, wrote, printed and sold the paper. Then we divided the profits. I remember one week we went after the hoodlum and gambling elements in the city. Were we the white haired boys, we got praise from all the pulpits in town. However, we spoiled our short-lived glory the next week by condemning the clergy for not having cleaned the town up before. As you might guess *Town Topics* soon died and I got a job on the *Vancouver Sun*.

Then I met Jack Voss in a bar and we began to talk. Over a beer we spoke of ships and crossing the Pacific in a small boat. From an imagined sea adventure it became a possibility when I agreed to buy a Siwash canoe and have it fitted to go to sea.

Mother wrote saying she thought the trip too dangerous, and my brother George came to try to persuade me not to go, but I think my Dad understood, his letters sounded both astonished and proud. [George wrote to his mother: Well Norm is at last gone. He left from Oak Bay at seven ten a.m. Norm's last words were in reference to the folks at home, and the last I heard of Norm was his gruff laugh coming across the water when he was half a mile from shore.]

Dangerous as were the storms and calms of the Pacific, they were as nothing compared to the clash of our personalities. Before we ever reached Apia, Samoa, we hated each other, and I was certain Voss intended to do me harm. It is a miracle to me that we two men, both strong-willed but of such different temperaments ever travelled ten thousand miles cooped up in the *Tilikum*.

I returned from Australia in 1902 and went to Calgary. I guess I was in poor shape because my friends sent me to Banff to recover. Well, dear girl, does this answer your questions—it seems a lot about little.

Dear little girl, you ask for more so I am going to try to tell you tonight once again, that in this whole world there is only one thing that I live for; have I not told you time and again that before I met you my life, my living was an existence only. That why I was born and existed I could never understand, that I cared little or nothing for life was only too true, for that I could prove to you in more ways than one. I lived with the world, that is I took all the pleasure that I enjoyed out of it; and even in time all that became tiresome and a bother. Often people asked me why I risked my life on the Pacific Ocean in a canoe. I have answered you that question in the above.

I went on that trip looking for what I did not know, but it was a great something that I knew I was without. That vacancy in my life had to be filled or else I cared not what became of me.

For a while I thought if I made lots of money that would bring me to the top of my ambitions. Well, dear, I made it in large sums but even then I was still without that terrible something and the money was no good to me. It only gave me a place in the world while it lasted, gave me friends that were no friends at all; and the day that my partner in the business in which we made the money skipped out—that day was a good friend to me. Often have I talked with my dear old mother, how I was sick of the life that I and all other people in my eyes at that time had to lead. She was a firm believer in God—the God you know—she told me to find Him, to learn and know Him and then I would be content. Do you know, dear, that I tried, oh so hard. Church, prayer, reading and talking with men who were wise in the church. A minister said, "Some day you will find God and He will make you understand."

Then I took that nightmare of a trip to Australia. On the trip I saw what a God-fearing man would call "God in all his might." Picture our trip in words I could not do. I have seen that old sailor [Voss] pray for nights and every night the storms were worse than the day before. I was in the water for hours with sharks around me as thick as trout in the Bow, yet, dear, do you think I could find that something that I never had in this life. Day after day brought new troubles and dangers, chased one day by a hundred canoes loaded with man-eating natives, next day starving for water, then all but crushed out of sight by a whale. Does this sound like a cheap dime novel, dear, well it is all true. Did all this bring me that for which I went to seek? Did this bring me to the God that I was taught was Love? No, dear, I could not put it down to God's might, it was only nature having her way and we had to beat it. I could only see that what I had been doing without all my life was not to be found in the South Sea Islands or Australia.

Once more, dear, I found myself at home among two or three of my good old friends, who all thought I was surely going to die, for I guess I looked pretty bad after the time I had. They all advised Banff—so Banff I took—more I guess to please them than anything else. After Banff came Morley—and—I met you.

I can only compare your coming with one night when I was on the Pacific Ocean. All the winds were loose, thunder, lightning, rain, the waves were mountain high and cold was no name for it. For almost two days and two nights my comrade and I had been bailing water out of the boat to keep her from sinking. The last night was one of the worst I had ever lived. We had given up hope of ever coming out alive. Voss was trying to pray and I guess I was swearing at him good and plenty for not dipping the water out faster, when suddenly I lifted my head up with a dipper of water to throw overboard, I saw a little speck of light away over our bow. I knew it was not a star it was too dark for that, and it flashed on me in a second that it was a lighthouse. Well, dear, I let a yell out of me that made Voss forget his prayers and that he was going to die. It is needless to say we made the light safely and got into a pretty little bay where we could hear the storm raging outside and we could laugh at it all.

Well, dear, that light is yourself. My past life is that stormy ocean, where it goes on day after day rolling around, doing no good in its rolling—in which I had the feeling of having lost something I had never had. When it did come, though no one told me or gave it a name I knew it was so, for I felt it in every nerve and fibre of my body. Without you and love of God this world would not be a safe place for man or woman. What I would have been I shudder to think. You started me on the right road in thought if not in deed.

I give all, not a love of eighteen or twenty, but a love that has been a man's lifetime; and I say not good enough for you. In meeting you, accepting many of your thoughts, studying your life, I go into a world and life so new and so grand I feel ashamed—yet I know we will build all our lives for others as for ourselves.

Voss was a hardened seaman, mature, egotistical, with black moods; Luxton, the youthful journalist and adventurer, resourceful and vital. The wonder is not that they parted company, but that they remained together as long as they did, nursing their fears and resentments. Luxton had the newspaperman's eye for a good story and what could be more thrilling than to sail around the world in an Indian canoe? Accordingly he insisted on an agreement signed before a notary, that he should have all publishing rights. Then Voss went back on his word and drafted an account, subsequently published under the title of *The Venturesome Voyages of Captain Voss*. Because Voss's account was not wholly accurate Luxton wrote a journal based on his day-to-day diary. In his copy of the Voss book Luxton wrote:

Captain Voss got things badly mixed up and where his memory failed him he made fiction. He also took a lot of the experiences from Vancouver to Fiji and put them in his later voyages. He missed two wrecks we had, one a very bad one.

Remote though his career in Banff may seem from the voyage of the *Tilikum*, it illustrates the personality and character of the man who was really responsible for the journey that made Captain Voss famous. Trader, naturalist, entrepreneur, writer and friend of the Indians, Norman appears in the pages of Banff's history as a haberdasher, as the owner of The Sign of the Goat Trading Post and as a taxidermist who shipped big game heads, furs, Indian beadwork and buckskin goods of all kinds everywhere in the world, to royalty, millionaires, hunters and tourists. In 1903 he wrote:

I have almost finished the store, dear girl, I shall call it the Sign of the Goat and I shall make it look like a museum so people will be interested, even if they do not always buy. I can see you shake your head about that, dear, but I like people. I am sure I shall make friends from all over the world, and I shall give credit. I know that I won't lose. [His files of correspondence show that this came true, for all the years he ran the store until shortly before his death.]

Norman always retained his interest in newspaper work, so when Banff's first newspaper failed, he bought the press. He published the *Crag and Canyon* which he operated himself from 1902 until 1951. He always reserved the right to compose the editorials, even when he had an editor, so he could criticize any person neglectful of his duties, member of parliament or the man in the street. Early in 1904 he wrote:

The King Edward Hotel should be running very soon. Dear girl, you don't realize I need to have plenty of business to give you the things I want to when we are married. I know that one day Banff will be a great summer and winter resort, and when the hotel is finished I shall throw the key away so the doors may never be closed.

Despite the loss by fire of the hotel February 7, 1914, and the livery barns shortly after, he promptly constructed the Lux Block containing a new hotel, several stores, and a moving picture theatre. With the passing of the horses Norman converted his business to automobiles and provided the first sightseeing cars for tourists.

Throughout his whole life Norman Luxton was a strong advocate of Banff as "The Playground of The Canadian Rockies." As early as 1906 he published a booklet entitled *Fifty Switzerlands in One— Banff the Beautiful*, which was sent all over the world.

I remember one evening in 1919 when Barny W. Collison, who was Stipendiary Magistrate in Banff, dropped in for a chat. We got talking of Banff's future and I told him of an idea I had for a Banff Winter Carnival. We talked until the small hours, and next day sent a telegram to Ottawa. The reply came back that the Government would back the project to the extent of five hundred dollars in labour and ice. After that for many years people came from all over the United States as well as Canada. The Canadian Pacific Railway ran special trains from Winnipeg, Edmonton and Vancouver. In 1923 we had the Hundred Mile Championship Sleigh Dog Race on Lake Minnewanka—the only time in its history it was not at Le Pas, Manitoba. Strongheart, the Wonder Dog of the movies, was making a picture in Banff at the time, and donated the Strongheart Trophy.

Lake Minnewanka, only nine miles from Banff, was a natural beauty spot to give pleasure to both tourists and local people. I decided to put a large, wood-burning boat, built like a steamer, on the lake in the summer and an ice boat in the winter, and I built a Chalet on the south shore. When the lake level was to be raised by the construction of the Calgary power dam I had a big supper party there, then we burned the Chalet. However, when the lake was to be raised a second time I moved the new Chalet into town and left Lake Minnewanka to Jack Stanley and his boat, which he had built in opposition to mine.

Even more than his business enterprises, Norman Luxton's name is associated in Alberta history with the Stoney Indians at Morley. From his boyhood days, when, with his father, he had met Louis Riel in the United States and had served his apprenticeship at the Indian Agency at Rat Portage, he was a friend of the Indians.

When the influenza epidemic in 1918 hit the Reserve I went to try to save as many of the Indians at Morley as I could. I wired the Superintendent-General of Indian Affairs at Ottawa outlining the desperate straits of the

Stonies. In reply I was told to do what I could. I organized burial parties, took food and supplies from my store in Morley and drove hundreds of miles over the Reserve visiting and revisiting the sick, giving them whisky and aspirin, the only two medicines available.

Not a word of thanks or any compensation did he ever receive from the federal authorities. Norman, himself, was taken ill with the influenza, but he had the satisfaction of knowing that he had saved the Stoney tribe at Morley. For these efforts and for his support of the Indian Association of Alberta in its efforts to obtain more land for the Stonies, Luxton was taken into the Stoney tribe as "Chief White Shield." The Blackfeet, too, honoured him with the rank and title of "Chief White Eagle." The Banff Indian Days between 1909 and 1950 were the result of his efforts and each year at the Calgary Exhibition and Stampede the Indians readily admitted his fairness when he judged the Indian section of the great parade and the teepees in the Indian village in the Fair Grounds.

In 1910 I was talking to Frank Oliver, then Member of Parliament for Edmonton and member of the Royal Conservation Commission, and suggested that the Canadian Government should buy one thousand buffalos from the herd belonging to Michael Pablo at Flat Head Lake in Montana. My suggestion met with approval and I opened negotiations to buy them for ninety dollars per head and have them shipped to Wainwright National Park. I'll never forget that trip—it was great.

Thus, through the foresight and imagination of one man, Norman Luxton, the buffalo came back to Canada. As he grew older, he became particularly interested in the conservation of wild animals and he enjoyed nothing better than getting into a canoe and paddling miles down rivers and through lakes taking count of the wild animals or the wild fowl for Ducks Unlimited, of which he was a member.

During his last years Norman was able to realize a dream of long standing, the Luxton Museum. With financial assistance from the Glenbow Foundation he brought together his lifetime collection of Indian artifacts, weapons, buckskins, beadwork and conveyances and arranged them so they would depict the life of the Prairie Indians. The first log building of the museum, the old Banff Gun Clubhouse, was one of the many log buildings and homes in Banff constructed by Luxton himself.

On November 2, 1904, he married Georgia Elizabeth McDougall, daughter of the well-known trader and rancher, David McDougall. She was a pioneer and native daughter, the first white child born in what is now Alberta, then part of the North West Territories. Because of her interest in the Indians, when she managed her father's trading post and through her later life, Mrs. Luxton was taken into the Stoney tribe as Princess and Blood-Sister. The Indians gave her the name of "Rainbow Woman" because, they explained, she always brought peace after the storm.

A slight man, five-foot-seven, Norman remained through his life wiry and resilient. His step was springy, his reactions quick, his temper uncertain, his blue eyes piercing yet always with laughter in them. His two-inch-brimmed round Stetson hats, specially made for him, were so much part of him they became symbolic. He was a steadfast friend to young and old alike and generous to anyone in need. For a man of action he was an omnivorous reader of history, travel and Indians.

On October 26, 1962, Norman Kenny Luxton, newspaperman, hunter, trader, adventurer and sailor died in Calgary. He was buried in his beloved Banff, while at the graveside the Indians, dressed in full ceremonial beaded costumes, held a special service. Missing from the many people from all over Canada who attended the funeral, was Jack Voss with whom he had set sail in the *Tilikum* sixty-one years before.

JOHN CLAUS VOSS

Many newspaper articles have been written about the *Tilikum* and her fabulous voyage, but these articles have said little or nothing about Captain John Claus Voss. He has been given as many nationalities as the *Tilikum* has been given Indian tribes who were supposed to have built her. Voss has been called a Swede, Dane, Norwegian and German, in various articles in the *Daily Colonist*, Victoria, B.C., the *Vancouver Province*, the *Sunday Province*, Vancouver, B.C., the *Minneapolis Tribune*, Minneapolis, Minnesota. The writers of these stories have said he sailed the ocean, that he prospected in Nicaragua until driven out by a revolution, that he was proprietor of a hotel in Victoria, that he drove a jitney in Tracy, California, and that he was a sealer. Some say he sailed away from Yokohama and was lost in 1913, others that he died in Tracy, California, in 1922. All this over the years from 1926 to 1961. The accounts of Voss neither agree nor do they provide clues as to where they obtained their information. Most of the writers who have referred to Voss have drawn most of their information from *The Venturesome Voyages of Captain Voss*.

Luxton's brother George wrote in a letter to his mother, dated Victoria, May 26, 1901, "Captain Voss, the sailor with whom Norm is going is an old experienced seaman, is married and has four children, two boys and two daughters, a great man for 'spinning yarns,' just the kind of rollicking Jack Tar with a sailor's roll. . . ."

The *British Columbia Directory*, 1895, refers to Voss and Perry, Queen's Hotel, corner of Johnson and Store Streets. There are further references in 1897 to J. C. Voss, prop. Queen's Hotel; 1898, J. C. Voss, prop. Queen's Hotel and Hotel Victoria, corner Johnson and Government Streets; 1898 and 1899, J. C. Voss, prop. Queen's Hotel and Hotel Victoria, Pandora Avenue; 1899–1900, Voss, J. C., prop. Queen's Hotel; Voss and Leason, props. Hotel Victoria; 1900–01, Voss, J. C., prop. Queen's Hotel. In 1901 the Queen's Hotel is given as the property of R. B. McClelland; J. C. Voss's name is not mentioned. The address of Mrs. J. C. Voss is listed as 9 Oscar Street.

Captain John Claus Voss was twice nominated for a Fellowship in the Royal Geographical Society, in June 1905 and again in March 1914. On both occasions he is described on the nomination forms as "Master Mariner." He did not, however, officially become a member or Fellow of the Society, for reasons that are obscure.

In his story of the *Xora*, Voss tells us, "My seafaring life commenced in the year of 1877, when I was quite a young man, and was spent up to the time I sailed in the *Xora*, in large sailing vessels, during which period I had filled all sorts of positions from deck boy to master."

Weston Martyr, a man who knew the sea, in his introduction to the second edition of *The Venturesome Voyages*, says that he met Voss first on the beach of Table Bay, Cape Town, South Africa; and when Voss told him he had got the *Tilikum* in Victoria and had sailed over via Sydney and Auckland, Martyr went on his way thinking, "That's only a very small man; but, by Jove, he's certainly a monumental liar!" It was not until 1912–13 that Martyr again saw Voss. After listening to him and witnessing the return of the *Sea Queen* after coming through the typhoon of August 3, 1919, Martyr talked with the crew, and became convinced of Voss's skill as a seaman and his veracity as a teller of tales. Martyr wrote of him:

Like most men who have done great things, Voss was not a satisfying talker. He had been too busy all his life to have time to acquire those qualities which we leisured, softer and less effectual folk call refinement and culture. . . . Be this as it may, a little "culture" is very helpful in enabling one to express one's thoughts, and expressing his thoughts was not . . . one of Voss's strong points. . . . At first he [Voss] would not talk; eventually the warmth of our hero worship thawed him and he commenced to summon spirits for us from the vast deep. . . . I fear we spoiled him: and in the end I heard it hinted that Voss spoke, perhaps, too much. I think one day he realized this himself. Suddenly he ceased to talk altogether. . . . For myself I can only say that I have found every word of Voss's concerning ships and the sea to be pure gold. . . . To this teaching I know I owe, at any rate, my life.

When Luxton read Martyr's impressions he wrote:

Everything Martyr says is true. Voss had such a poor way of telling things he discredited himself. Ten times more than Martyr's praise would not cover Voss's abilities. Voss knew the sea. He knew what to do at the right time and he did it. He always *never* took a chance and quit the sealing game in Bering Sea for that reason. It was too rough. As a sailor there was never anyone quite so wonderful; winds, weather, water, currents, dead reckoning, he had no equal in his time.

According to Norman Luxton, Voss claimed to be a Dane and frequently referred to childhood incidents and early memories when they talked during the long hours in the *Tilikum*. Luxton did not feel that the John Voss, whose obituary record is at Tracy, California, could be the same Voss, not only because of discrepancies as to years of residence or nationality, but because he believed Voss was not the kind of man who would settle down to drive a taxi. Luxton was convinced that Voss had died in his element, in the yawl that left Yokohama in 1913 to cross the Pacific. One cannot help feeling that Captain Voss would have asked nothing better than to have ended his days in the sea he loved so well and sailed so bravely. This may explain why his election to the Royal Geographical Society was not carried through in 1914. Nevertheless there must always remain an element of doubt as to whether the John C. Voss of Germany, who died of pneumonia at Tracy on February 27, 1922, whose occupation is given on his certificate of death as "Captain, Sea Boat," might have been the man who sailed with Luxton in the *Tilikum*.

CANOE *TILIKUM*

In the year 1901, May 20, the *Tilikum* set sail from Victoria, B.C., on the first leg of her journey around the world. She followed a course which took her from Vancouver Island to Tahiti, Samoa and Fiji, on to Australia and New Zealand, then to Cape Town, across the Atlantic to Pernambuco, to the Azores and finally to the Thames River, England, September 2, 1904. The vessel making this remarkable voyage was a Siwash Indian dugout, thirty feet in length, built from a single red cedar log and at least a hundred years old. According to her Indian owner, the dugout had been in many Indian battles on the West Coast of British Columbia. Despite her background of war and violence, the vessel was given the name *Tilikum*, a Chinook word meaning "friend."

During the voyage to the South Pacific the crew of the *Tilikum* consisted of John Voss, captain, and Norman Luxton, mate. The latter had purchased the canoe and met the expenses incurred to make her seaworthy, after Voss had persuaded the Indian owner to sell. Prior to the departure of the *Tilikum* from Oak Bay, Victoria, Norman Luxton and his brother George sailed the *Tilikum* on a trial run. In a letter to his mother George wrote:

All day last Saturday [May 19, 1901] I was sailing in Norm's *Tilikum*, she sails like a fish. When we were about ten miles we struck some pretty heavy seas. . . . We went right across to the American shore. I was going to land but the tide was running out so heavily the boat could not get close enough in to enable me to reach the shore. She stands rough weather fine. Before we got back to Victoria the wind was blowing something terrible, the waves were rolling something awful, we rolled up and down as if we were on a gigantic rocking horse. Sometimes the boat would nearly stand on end, but we did not take any water and we could not upset because there was so much ballast on board. Oh! It was just fine, so exhilarating.

After her feat of sailing around the world, the *Tilikum* had one brief moment of glory when she was exhibited at Earl's Court, London, England, during the Navy and Marine Exhibition in 1905. Then the gallant canoe was left to rot for some twenty-odd years in a ship graveyard in the Thames, neglected by all except the seagulls.

In 1928 or 1929 it seems that a group of British naval officers at Sheerness were discussing various types of craft and their seaworthiness. One of them stated that Vancouver Island Indian canoes were among the best and drew attention to the *Tilikum*, then grounded on a tidal flat on Canvey Island. According to information obtained from the National Maritime Museum, Greenwich, one of these officers went to look at the derelict and wrote to Mr. H. T. Barnes of Victoria, British Columbia. When Barnes received this information, he got in touch with George I. Warren of the Victoria Publicity Bureau. Warren then wrote to W. A. McAdam, agent-general at British Columbia House in London, asking him to investigate. He inserted an advertisement in the *Yachting Times* asking for information about the *Tilikum* and within about two weeks received word from the brothers, E. W. Byford and A. Byford, who stated that they were the owners of the hull. The Byford brothers agreed to give the *Tilikum* to Victoria provided she would not be exhibited for gain and provided that the city and the Vancouver Island Publicity Bureau would assume the expenses of returning her to Victoria. The outcome of these various letters was the return of the hull of the *Tilikum* to the city from which she had set out on her memorable voyage.

When the *Tilikum* arrived in Victoria, the question was: where should she be displayed? H. F. Matthew, manager of the Empress Hotel, offered a site beside the Crystal Garden, near the Legislative Building. The Victoria Chamber of Commerce, after canvassing a number of business firms, made a few repairs to the vessel and on August 7, 1930, placed her on display. Six years later the Thermopylae Club of Victoria undertook the task of restoring her to something like her original condition. This was done at a cost of two hundred dollars. The money was raised by passing a hat at a meeting of the British Columbia Historical Society and the work was undertaken by Captain Victor Jackobsen, a former sealing schooner skipper. Not only was the *Tilikum* more or less restored, she was also given a new resting place in Thunderbird Park in 1940. No provision, however, was made for protection and by 1944 she was again in a sorry state. In that year the provincial government placed a fence around her and a roof over her.

In 1965, when plans were being made for a new provincial museum, the provincial authorities asked Colonel J. W. D. Symons, director of the Maritime Museum of British Columbia, if he would give the *Tilikum* a home since she would have to be moved from her location to make way for the new provincial museum building. The trustees of the Maritime Museum agreed and a portion of the museum wall was broken down to permit the entry of the vessel into the building. Here the *Tilikum* has remained for all to see since June 8, 1965. Although sharp questions were asked in Victoria at the time about the fact that the vessel was being placed in a museum which charged an entrance fee, objections diminished in number and volume and subsided when it was made clear that the museum was a registered nonprofit society and the *Tilikum* was not being displayed for gain.

The vessel, as she may be seen at the present time, is not exactly as she was when Voss and Luxton sailed her in the South Pacific. The figurehead, which Norman Luxton carved, was kicked by a horse in Pretoria, South Africa, and was broken. It was replaced by a new and slightly different one. When she was abandoned on Canvey Island the stem rotted and once again the figurehead was lost. One of wood and metal was part of the restoration carried out by the Thermopylae Club. Today the cabin, cockpit, deck fittings and a hand-carved figurehead, an exact replica of Norman Luxton's, are restored so the *Tilikum* once more appears as she was when she set out from Victoria on that May morning in 1901.

The enclosed notes are more like half forgotten dreams than actual happenings. Those who read must remember that more than a quarter of a century had passed before I commenced to put my thoughts in writing. Many adventures of this trip may have been forgotten, but those that are told are in no way embellished. So from a poor memory and a badly kept diary I dedicate these manuscripts to my good friends Dexter and Winchester, and also it is an answer to a published book called *The Venturesome Voyages of Captain Voss*.

—N. K. LUXTON
*Written in Banff during
the winter of 1927–28*

I

*Buying and Preparing
the Canoe*

*Something to do about buying and making the canoe
ready, also the collecting of skulls and grave relics.*

In my mind the image is as clear as if I saw it yesterday, yet
twenty-eight years have passed since the month of April 1901.
The wee cove was land-bound. On three sides were delightful
sand and stone beaches, while an abrupt rock shore rose on the
ocean side, forming an entrance so small two men (one on each side)
armed with ten foot teepee poles could have closed it to any boat trying to enter. The cove was absolutely storm proof and almost rain
proof because the boughs of the trees bent far over the water. Many,
many years ago these great cedars had seen explorers and Spanish
ships pass along through what is now called Queen Charlotte Straits.

Could two damn fools find a more perfect setting for what they
were preparing for? No, not if they had looked over the entire coast of
Vancouver Island. These preparations were for an adventure that
would no doubt have been refused by more experienced seamen than

Captain John Voss. Yet a mighty seaman he was, born hundreds of years after his time, delayed for some unaccountable reason in the Unknown. A Viking who belonged to the ages before Christ yet born in the nineteenth century. A man out of place; the butt of those who thought they knew the sea, and a great wonder to all who read his adventures; later to command the admiration of poofers and know-alls.

In that little inlet, one of nature's wonders barely eighty by forty feet, I can still see a red cedar dugout canoe, anchored, but bobbing up and down with the ripple of the North Pacific roll. Of British Columbian Indian make and all of a hundred years old, the identity of that canoe would have stayed with it as easily as the identities of famous old warships of the British Navy. Without doubt the canoe, if she could write, would tell of many bloody fights, of total extermination of Siwash tribes surprised in their sleep. Only by hard talking and the display of eighty silver dollars was Captain Voss able to secure the relic from an ancient Siwash woman. Why? Because it was in this hundred-year-old cedar tree that Captain John Voss and Norman Kenny Luxton, newspaperman (myself), had decided by cold reasoning and sea-knowledge that we would cross the Pacific Ocean.

John Voss had learned his seamanship in perhaps the most cruel waters on the face of old Mother Earth, the North Sea. A Dane by birth, Jack could not tell just how young he was when he first remembered the ocean, wind, and boats. In early manhood he had several times rounded Cape Horn and not an ocean or sea in the world had he not sailed. Is it any wonder that he had little or no trouble to persuade a young Canadian man, born on the prairies of Manitoba before the Canadian Pacific Railway ever entered the West, to embark on a trip of adventure, one that was never to man's knowledge ever taken before and one possibly that will never be repeated in a craft so small? Yet so confident were we that such a trip could be made, never in our many talks when preparing the boat for sea was there even the slightest word passed of possible failure.

For the best part of a month this old hull was worked on with the assistance of a carpenter. The sides were built up seven and a half inches, held in place by one inch square oak ribs, bent to run from bow to stern twenty-four inches apart from top to bottom inside the canoe. Inside, two-by-four joists or floor timbers were fastened, over which was laid a kelson of the same dimensions. A keel of oak three by eight inches on the outside bottom of the canoe was bolted to the keelson, then three hundred and eighty pounds of lead were fastened to the bottom of the keel. All this was to prevent the canoe from breaking or splitting, the keel and keelson sandwiched the bottom of the canoe, and the ribs crossed the natural grain of the long sides and bottom. The keel was some twenty-eight feet, the overall some thirty-two feet, about a five foot beam and the depth of thirty-six inches. Ten feet from the bow a water-tight bulkhead was built with a floor hatch on the deck. Directly after this came the cabin of about eight feet in length. About fourteen feet from the bow bulkhead came an aft bulkhead, also water-tight. Immediately in front of this aft bulkhead there were two galvanized water tanks under the cockpit or well, and their fore ends were flush with the hatch that led into the cabin from the cockpit so that they formed part of the aft end of the cabin well. These tanks were built to the shape of the sides of the canoe and were held in place by two inch square pieces of wood resting on the floor joists. These tanks together held about eighty gallons of water. Immediately aft and behind the wash board of the cockpit came the aft hatch just in front of which was the mizzenmast, and through the centre of the cabin came the mainmast. The fore mast was just fore of the cabin wall and fore of the mast came the fore hatch. The bow of the canoe to the end of the bowhead reached some seven feet. With a jib sail, foresail, mainsail and spanker, all her canvas would hardly measure two hundred twenty-five square feet. Peak and throat halliards all trailed back to the starboard outside of the wash board of the cockpit, snubbed over small wooden cleats; the sheets down the port side of the canoe were held in the same way. Thus a man sitting in the cockpit at the helm could in a moment let every running gear on the canoe loose. The masts were all secured by small thin steel wires. Ballast was put beneath the floor boards, to the extent of six hundred pounds, and effectively held in place by the floor. Four small sacks of sand were usually kept in the cockpit to trim ship.

Some thousand dollars outfitted the canoe, provisions consisting of: canned goods of all descriptions, hard tack, a few vegetables, cooking outfits, a medicine chest, and a wee stove, which burnt the blocks of well-seasoned resins, wood was fastened to the end of the bunk; a thirty-thirty and a forty-four Winchester rifle, a sixteen bore shotgun, and a Stevens twenty-two long barrelled pistol, a camera and two gross of plates, a sextant with the mirror cracked and partly gone, a small spirit compass and for a chronometer, a Waltham watch P. S. Bartlett no. 2850606, which lost one-fifth of a second every twenty-four hours, a *South Pacific Directory* of 1884 print and one chart of the Pacific Ocean, both bought in a second-hand store. Thus was this old Siwash war canoe ready for her adventurous voyage. Rechristened the *Canoe Tilikum*, meaning in the Chinook language "friend," and registered at the Port of Victoria as the *Pelican* (I find that Voss registered it as the *Pelican*, why I do not know[1]).

While I was not helping to re-model the canoe and when work had become stale, I was by no means idle. Through my carving and imagination the figurehead on the bowsprit came into being which even among the native American Indians was a source of wonder. All through the South Seas the lagoon folks still talk of the boat with a head whose mother was a sea serpent and whose father was a bird, and carried in its pit the heads of dead men on which to feed.

---

[1] Luxton wrote elsewhere he thought Voss registered the *Tilikum* as the *Pelican* to throw the American authorities off his trail when he left Canada.

Digging in the sand one day for iron gravel to ballast the canoe I came across a most wonderful brass cannon with very old markings which proved its Spanish origin. Hardly twenty inches long and with a bore for muzzle loading two inches in diameter, it was quite as good as the day some venturesome landing party had lost it. Proudly this was mounted to the bottom of the fore hatch of the *Tilikum*, so that with the release of a catch and a flip of the fore hatch the cannon came up to a position ready for firing.

Toward the north end of Queen Charlotte Straits some two miles from the mainland is an island. The west side is almost perpendicular but on the mainland side are many shelving terraces. On these terraces, in canoes of all lengths and ages lay the forefathers of the Indians of today. On a moonless night, gliding silently, would come a fleet of war canoes to surprise the sleeping village. Man, woman and child were slaughtered except perhaps a very small number who escaped into the forest. Later these came back to bury their dead. The sacred island became over-crowded and had not been used for a hundred years when I came there.

I had found a field of research I was particularly interested in from a scientific angle, so without permit from either Indians or government I took pictures and collected artifacts. Many a night, while Voss waited quietly at the oars, I worked. The Indians in the village on Vancouver Island did not appreciate my point of view and one night they lay in wait for me. Their religious beliefs would not allow them to land on the island, day or night, so they kept their canoes a few hundred feet from the perpendicular shore. They waited patiently until I appeared on the skyline. Bang! Bang! Bullets zipped all around me, the hunter of heads, from a dozen shots. I had just got my load, a skull hooked by the cheekbone in one hand and a bag with artifacts in the other, ready to return to Voss. I needed no second invitation to leave and in my haste fell into the largest canoe I had yet discovered.

A few nights later I returned to that canoe and in it made a find I have never since repeated. It was a large, wild goat hair blanket. The hair had been roughly made into a rope. This was then woven together by an endless interlocking stitch. The robe and a number of skulls I carefully stowed away in the *Tilikum* before she left for the broad Pacific, to be used one day in the centre of the ocean to save both boat and crew. Photographs of the burial ground and the mis-shapen[2] skulls went to Ottawa. The artifacts went to many museums where they are today. Death and extinction stalked so closely to those Indians of hundreds of years ago that they had no time to develop and preserve their arts. Unfortunately these have long since gone into oblivion.

---

[2] It was the custom of the Indian mothers of that time to bind the heads of infants very tightly. This resulted in elongated narrow skulls.

37

II

Village Islands

*Something to do with smuggling in the early days along
the Pacific coast. Adverse weather and storm
bound and much to do with Indians at Village Islands.*

It was an ideal morning that Voss and I and the carpenter left our little cove to sail the *Tilikum* to Victoria before a wind that gradually freshened into a good stiff blow, so that before reaching Oak Bay wharf Captain Voss had changed the ballast to some four hundred pounds heavier. Here at Victoria the carpenter was paid off. Early morning, May 20, 1901, after an all night dance at the Dallas Hotel, I joined the *Tilikum* at Oak Bay. Five friends, including relatives[3] were there to see the venture off, so quiet had the proposed voyage been kept, but not so quiet that the American Navy Coast Guard had not heard, and as I found out later, had for thirty days

---

[3]   Captain Voss's wife, daughter, young son; O. B. Ormond, Victoria (Ormond's Biscuits); George Luxton, Minneapolis, Minn. (brother of Norman).

searched the Strait of Juan de Fuca for the *Tilikum* while the boat was trying to beat its way from Vancouver Island waters.[4] The American gunboat eventually piled itself on some rocks and no doubt cost Uncle Sam thousands of dollars more than the *Tilikum* was worth. These American Coast Guards had an idea Voss was one of nineteen still out of some California penitentiary, where they had been sent for increasing the population of the United States with Chinamen, without the proper entry. Anyhow, they wanted Voss. Voss, apparently, was not anxious to meet them, as the course of the *Tilikum* was not set to take in Honolulu on her trip across the Pacific. Voss's experience along the Pacific coast in early days was thrilling to say the least, and up to the time before we began hating each other's company and were on speaking terms, Voss passed whole watches away recounting smuggling experiences of earlier days, Chinamen to California and opium back to Vancouver Island.

For instance, a captain with eight or a dozen Chinamen bound for California need never be caught. Of course, his papers and manifests were a side issue, the real cargo being the Chinamen. It seems a wise captain kept on deck several large bags, eight feet long at

---

[4] Letter from George Luxton to his mother, Victoria, B.C., May 26, 1901. "There is quite a little story connected with Norm's leaving. There has been quite a bit of 'dope' smuggling between United States and Victoria. Well the United States government got wise and set watches on the *Tilikum*. On Sunday the U.S.S. *Grant*, a revenue cutter, arrived at Victoria. When I got back from seeing Norm off, I looked in at the dock and the U.S.S. *Grant* was gone! Four days after she again came in, this time surrounded by half a dozen barges to prevent her from sinking. The plain facts were the *Grant* had an eye on Voss and wasted two or three weeks running up and down the coast waiting for the *Tilikum* to leave and when she was in United States waters . . . they would search her. . . . Evidently the *Grant* . . . struck a rock, made a hole about ten feet across her bottom, the sailors had to take to the boats and the whole thing will cost Uncle Sam about $1500 and all for nothing."

least, with potatoes in them, and many empty large sacks. Then perhaps came the time when he was being overtaken by a gunboat, the warning cannon shot had been passed across the bow of his schooner. The Chinamen, all about frightened to death were out of sight, crouched down behind the bulwark. They would do anything the captain would tell them. Each Chinaman got into an empty sack, the sack then was tied tight with the idea that they would be covered up with the sacks full of potatoes. The captain, it seems, had a better plan to hide them. He did not use the potatoes. Down came a section of the bulwark of the schooner and then to each sack of Chinamen as he pulled it to the gaping hole of the railing, the captain hung a hundred pound shot. When overboard each shot went straight to the bottom carrying with it the bag of human freight. The gunboat crew came up, manifest and papers were all in order, thus would a captain of no conscience escape, and save his boat for another venture and his soul for Hell.

After dancing all night I immediately went below, leaving Voss to take the first watch. It was not until Race Rocks, ten miles from Victoria, when the rip tide started in to show the *Tilikum* what it could do with a small boat, that I woke up. A head wind did not improve matters and here Voss found the *Tilikum* was not so good on the wind. Tack for tack was made all day with very few miles astern. As night was fast coming on and the *Tilikum* had the floor boards of the cabin good and wet and showing at least five inches of water through the ballast, the captain decided to pull into Sooke Harbour, a few miles west of Race Rocks. Here the boat was beached at high tide as the leaks had caused some concern, and a thorough examination was made. Nothing could be seen that would account for one single drop of water. The conclusion was arrived at that while the boat was easing herself over each wave part of her entire hull would be out of water and with some strain to her hull. The natural splits or grain of the log would open and shut. This apparently was the reason

40

for the leakage, because always after throughout the entire voyage when she was riding high and mighty there was always bailing to be done. Having given her bottom a good coat of copper paint which dried very quickly in the hot sun, once more on the return tide the *Tilikum* shaped her course for the Pacific and with a fair wind this time got well under Cape Flattery so that Flattery Bay could be seen from the canoe. Suddenly, the wind changed to the southwest with nasty looking weather behind it. Voss refused to go into Flattery Bay, but sailed toward Vancouver Island on the Canadian side. The weather increased to a fury and fogged up until visibility was less than a quarter of a mile. To make matters worse, Voss got his usual sea-sick spell that came with every gale, and I took the tiller. Fortunately I did, because inside of half an hour when it was almost dark I recognized the entrance into San Juan Inlet. Otherwise it would have been a case of fight the storm all night or blow back to Race Rocks. San Juan has fairly deep water but eventually the little twenty-five-pound anchor found a holding and while Voss took the locker for a bunk I occupied the real bunk. This was the first night the crew had both slept on board. One bunk in the cabin was all that was necessary for when sailing the watches were six hours on and six hours off, the clock around.

Next morning the crew decided to go to visit John Baird,[5] Mrs. Baird, and their little girl, who lived at the head of the inlet. A few minutes' sail landed the *Tilikum* at their wharf. Needless to say John Baird, who was an old friend of my Winnipeg days, did his best to persuade me not to venture on so foolish a voyage, even offering me an interest in his cedar forest holding if I would stay and forget so mad a venture. I compromised, and accepted a five gallon jug of buttermilk and promised to see John on my return home, which I did. So, once more pointing

---

[5]   *Electoral District Voters' List*, Esquimalt, 1900. "Baird, Joseph John: Farmer, San Juan River."

her nose to the broad and blue Pacific, the *Tilikum* sailed away, Voss said, at six miles an hour. In the afternoon land was all but out of sight, but toward evening the wind hauled well around to the south.

Voss asked me if I had ever been in Alberni Inlet and on being assured that I knew this part of the coast well, the *Tilikum* once more was driven back to her native shores, this time before a howling gale. Late that night the boat was anchored behind Cape Beal Lighthouse, and so tired were the two of us that we dropped to sleep without change or food. After breakfast we upped anchor and sailed over to Dodge Cove,[6] five miles from Beal Lighthouse and a snug place to anchor inside Alberni Inlet. Here, in front of two Indian villages, the *Tilikum* rested for long days. Here we met dear old Mr. McKenzie,[7] an old country Scotsman and Indian trader, and to the bosom of his family (the cat and Mac) he took the *Tilikum* crew. Nothing was too good for us. His house, his cooking, and his friendship were all ours. Already I had been asked by Indians for whisky, hardly before our anchor was down, but the *Tilikum* only carried the spirits of her departed warriors. Naturally the begging Indians had been refused, but after going up to Mac's house he happened to look through the window and there on board the *Tilikum* was an Indian with Mrs. John Baird's demi-john of buttermilk to his mouth. He soon dropped it, and if action spoke disgust this Indian was all that. Buttermilk must have been a new beverage for him. These Indians

---

[6] See *British Columbia Gazetteer*, 1909. Dodge Cove is undoubtedly Dodger Cove, which is described as being "on the north of Diana Island, Barkley Sound, west coast of Vancouver Island." It is now known as Dodger Channel, see *British Columbia Gazetteer*, 1953 and 1966.

[7] *British Columbia Directory*, 1897 to 1902, lists under Dodger Cove, "McKenzie, M.J.: general store." The storekeeper at Dodger Cove would have been Murdoch James McKenzie, who is listed in the *Voters' List*, 1900, as being "a merchant at Dodger Cove," and in the *Voters' List*, 1903 and 1907, as being "a merchant at Ucluelet."

have a most peculiar way of showing their appreciation of a drink. If I or Voss had complied with the wishes of these Indians that morning they, the Indians, would have seized the canoe and crew, run her to Port Alberni, laid a complaint, and collected half the fine, anything from fifty to five hundred dollars, whatever the judge might impose.

This part of Alberni Inlet is known as Village Islands. In 1901, besides McKenzie's trading store, the village supported a government school for Indian children, and two villages of some forty or fifty houses, wonderfully furnished according to the success the owner might have had in seal hunting the previous season. Here many of the old sealing schooners found their seal hunters and many long pow-wows and talks to secure or persuade the Indians to join a vessel were held on the beaches in front of the villages by the sealing captains. Each schooner carried hunters to its accommodating capacity, two men or man and wife to a canoe with each team supplying its own canoe and sealing tackle when rifles were not used. Then to Bering Sea for three or four months' trip and return with a hold full of valuable seal skins. So much a hide was paid to the hunters, and thousands of dollars became the share of these Indians.

It was a common thing to see several sewing machines in one Indian house or half a dozen phonographs, and beds and tables by the dozen but never used. The floors of the houses or the beach were mostly used for domestic purposes. Invariably, dripping from huge slabs a foot by four feet long of blubber fat from the whales or black fish, the grease fell on all this display of wealth, amid smells reeking to the heavens. Dirty greasy children were always in evidence. Indeed the Siwash is not a model of the American races. If by chance the owner of the house should die, to ease his condition in the next world all these household goods were piled upon his grave, often including the very doors and window sashes of his house.

In these Village Islands, to me, these Indians appeared rougher and more assertive than in villages closer to Victoria and Vancouver.

Possibly it was the hard life they led for the sea had to give them their living and no savage grows less savage that lives by the sea in northern climates.

One day during the stay of the *Tilikum* at Village Islands a small Indian boy came to me and said his father wanted to see me. Following the boy I was led to one of the largest of the frame houses on the beach. Here in front of the house was a big Siwash Indian man dressed in nothing but a white cotton full dress shirt, whiling away time by smoothing the bottom of a huge dugout canoe with a pine torch. By flaming the bottoms of their canoes and then rubbing them with flat stones the canoes' surfaces take on a smooth and highly polished finish which causes them to slip through the water with greater ease. Apparently this Indian was making ready for a black fish hunt as all sorts of harpoons, lines and bladders were in evidence. He explained to me that he was a very sick man and on looking closer at him I discovered he was a mass of small boils with legs, arms, and trunk a network of running sores. I assured him that I could cure him if he would follow my directions and take the medicine I would send him but in return he must give me one whaling spear and shaft, and take me on the whale hunt he was preparing. The Indian readily agreed to the terms. All this was carried on in the Chinook language. I gave him a very strong purgative which he was to take for three days, also a soothing solution in which was a mild disinfectant to wash the sores. The next day I called for my harpoon but the patient was apparently much better so why pay this white man when there was nothing more to cure. But, lo and behold! the next day the Indian's wife appeared on the scene and assured me that her man was dying by "running away," such was the literal translation of her Chinook, and begged me to save her husband. I assured her the man would die and that nothing could save him. The harpoon was angry because it was kept in a boat it did not belong to and the whale hunt would not succeed as her husband had decided not to

44

include the white man. Away she rushed to her spouse with the news of his very soon decease, and apparently the Indian was thoroughly frightened for back came one of the very finest whale harpoons this mighty Indian hunter possessed, with a beautiful sixteen foot shaft of perfect balance and weight. With it came all the assurance of a whale hunt as soon as the weather permitted. Stowing away the harpoon on the *Tilikum*, I gave the squaw a remedy for "running away." But it really took the Indian five days to get back to normal, and not surprisingly the boils healed almost as rapidly.

Using my fame as a "Medicine Man" I got permission one morning to attend a gathering of friends of a very sick Indian youth. The friends were there to sing and wail while the tribe's Medicine Man removed great pains and sickness from the bladder and privates of the youth. Stretched on the ground on a blanket in quite a large dark hut lay the sickest Indian I have ever seen. Wasted to a shadow and suffering untold agony it was easy to see that no power available in that camp could help him. However the Medicine Man got busy. Dressed in a long dark flowing robe and with a very ugly painted red cedar face mask tied to his head, he suddenly appeared from a dark corner of the hut, announcing his presence with a blood-curdling yell which was immediately taken up by all the natives and friends present. It seemed to me that this horrible noise went on for an hour and all the time the Medicine Man was working around and hovering over the patient. Suddenly, with a howl that discounted anything offered before, the Medicine Man straightened up and in his hands was a round stone quite the size of a goose egg. This he showed to his admiring audience assuring them he had taken it from the belly of the sick youth. Strange to say for a few minutes the boy seemed to be better, but once more he relapsed into his moaning pain. Not to be discouraged, the Medicine Man, with reinforcements of more friends and more noise to frighten away the bad spirits, went at the stone removing again. All day long this ceremony continued until there was a pile of stones in the centre of the hut much larger than the patient. Every little while the Medicine Man would disappear into the dark corner of the hut, change his head dress and no doubt renew his supply of stones which he carefully concealed under his flowing garments. The youth did not die until the following morning. Faith in the old faker, with an equal faith in his friends, caused him to live past any reasonable time for such a terrible disease.

Not very far from one of the villages and quite in sight of the village on the opposite side of Dodge Cove, time and water from the sea had carved a long, low tunnel into the solid rock at the end of which was quite a good sized room. The tunnel was so low that a person had to get on his hands and knees to get through. Finding this place I explored, and in the room on natural rock shelves rested many bundles of dead Indians. These graves were fairly new and such being the case I had no desire to molest them, but decided that I would get some photographs of the death chamber and its furnishings. Going to the *Tilikum* I got my camera and some flash-powder and returned to the cave. Apparently the villagers across the cove had seen my movements for I had hardly set my camera in place and was just lighting one of the flashlights when I heard the scrambling sound of several bodies coming through the tunnel. It was quite apparent I would have some explaining to do, but wanting the picture I touched off a flashlight just as the "jury and judge" entered the burial chamber. A blinding flash, a report followed immediately by another, was quite sufficient for the company of Indians, and with loud cries of fright they disappeared into the tunnel. Who got to the boat first I at the time did not know, but fast time was made through this almost inaccessible passage. McKenzie afterwards told me that the man with no legs had won the race, so far in advance was he of the others that he had actually gotten into the boat and was pushing off so that the others had to wade to reach it. To my mind I had never met anything quite so repulsive in the human race as this crippled Indian with no legs. The nearest of anything he could be compared to would be that misbegotten character, the dwarf of Notre Dame. With feet and calves the size of a six-year-old baby, this Indian pulled himself around on his butt. He had a trunk much too small for a huge head that could never be still, and features and face of indescribable ugliness, with apparently a character to fit all his deformities. But such is the superstitious nature of these savages that after the cave experience of which I never heard any more a daily present of fresh fish was made at McKenzie's home for me by this cripple, yet he was known throughout the village as a man who never gave anything away in his life but always used his crippled state to beg and steal wherever he could.

The north village on the cove was watered by a year round spring stream which had for years supplied water to the Siwash families. For some unaccountable reason at the time of the *Tilikum*'s call, this spring was gradually drying up very much to the concern of the natives. One day McKenzie told me to go post myself behind a huge cedar tree close to the spring, there to stay, keep out of sight, make no noise and see what I would see.

Just how long I had been asleep on watch behind the tree I could not say but something disturbed me and I awakened. I all at once heard the voice of an Indian talking in the Siwash tongue. Quietly getting to my feet, I saw not six paces from the tree the old Medicine Man who had produced the many stones from the youth's belly, talking, but talking to no one that I could see. It was only by listening intently that I made out the meaning of a few words. It was afterwards when I saw McKenzie that I got the full meaning of the Indian's supplications. There the old fellow stood, dirty as he was he seemed to command a dignity that is hard to express. Bending over the tiny stream of water with his arms stretched wide before him, palms down, then suddenly straightening up, throwing wide his arms and face uplifted to the trees, he beseeched the stream to keep on

47

flowing. It had watered and kept from thirst the trees, the bushes, the flowers, the grass and the animals on all these islands for son after son of all his people. It had always been a friend so why now disappear when it had been a father and a mother for long ages to all the living things of the earth. If his people had in any way offended then he would search for the wrong-doers, and punishment even to death would follow. Baring his breast to the shadows of the forest, striking it hard with his hands or fists, then waving his arms up to the trees and sky, bending over again and again for nearly an hour, the old man made his plea. Apparently finally becoming exhausted he sank to the ground, and with slow tired motions he gathered his dirty blanket around his bare body and, to me, appeared to go to sleep.

It is my understanding that these old time Indians had no one particular god. Each thing on earth carried to them a being or spirit which could help or oppose them. For instance, this stream of water was in itself a spirit or it might be controlled by water spirits, so that with proper supplications and the most outrageous promises the Indian hoped to make the Water Spirit his friend. Indeed, it was a serious matter for the village if this spring ever dried up. It meant moving the entire tribe to another drinking place, and their houses would be a total loss. Once a year in olden days thanks were given by Indian tribes to all Nature. To prepare for this ceremony many Indians, both male and female, would starve themselves for days before the day of thanksgiving, abstaining from all food and water and preparing themselves, as they expressed it, to be less of the earth and more of the air. In this state of almost coma they were better prepared to help their fellow tribesmen out of sickness, and their understanding of the unknown was, to their way of thinking, more keen. In these Sun Dances, as they are called among prairie tribes, the Indian does not pray to any particular god. He gives thanks to the whole Universe, and in this case he seems to class them all under one spirit. This he calls the Great Spirit, which looks down on all the sky, the clouds, the sun, the moon and stars, the water, the trees, the grass and on all the animals and fishes. The Indian, believing that all things are controllable if he can only make his prayers strong enough, called it "His Medicine." It is well known history among Indian men of Western Canada, where urgent prayer was offered to the clouds for rain during some famous Sun Dances, that in many cases rain descended much to the wonderment of the whites but not in any way to the Indians. The idea of the rain was to cool the air and earth and to relieve the suffering of the fasting leaders of the ceremony. Otherwise they could not last long, it being the desire of the tribe to keep the thanksgiving going.

Close to this stream of water and behind one of the villages, I one day was walking through the forest returning from a duck hunt when much to my surprise I came upon a church building constructed of well-milled lumber and carrying a good sized tower. The window panes were intact but the door had dropped from its wrought iron hinges. The floor was very much broken and decayed, and growing through the broken boards were dozens of trees that reached to the sloping roof of the chapel. The pulpit was in good condition. Hanging over it, all faded and worn, were the remains of a surplice, and on top was a large Bible with its leaves rain swollen and mildewed. It was easy to see this place had not been occupied for years and of its history I could gather but little. But it seems that strong opposition, years before, had been given to this once Roman Catholic Mission,[8] so that the fathers had to move to more congenial villages.

8 *Daily Colonist* (Victoria, B.C.), April 26, 1890, p. 1: "Reverend Father Verbeke is at present in town on a brief visit, which is partly a holiday and partly a business trip. His primary object is to purchase lumber for the construction of a church at Dodger Cove. He will purchase the shingles and lining here, while the other material will be bought at Alberny. The little church, which is destined to be very prettily furnished, will be about twenty feet wide, with a centre aisle, and twenty-four feet long; this of course does not include the sanctuary, which will be about fourteen by fourteen feet."

III

A Whale Hunt

Killing time while storm bound. A frightened
sailing master. Luxton shanghaied by his old chum.
An exciting whale hunt.

It was the later part of May that the *Tilikum* blew in under and past Beal Light, and it was not until the 6th of July, 1901 that she eventually got under way to the Pacific for keeps. Weather conditions for most of June were the worst that the coast had experienced for years. Mail and passenger boats to Port Alberni from Victoria or elsewhere were all cancelled. It seemed I and Voss had much time on our hands. Voss employed himself by pulling out and putting back the *Tilikum*'s stores. The damp soaked continually through the inch thick sides of the soft cedar canoe so that stores, closed in the dark holds of a boat with no air or sun, soon swelled up and became useless, and it was only the constant handling, airing, and sunshine that made it possible for the stores to be saved at all. I spent most of my time exploring the surrounding country either by foot or canoe, but I did not find any more old burial places to collect from. One day I did find the dance hall for all the surrounding tribes, a huge log building seventy feet long and forty feet wide. In this place were stored some wonderfully made canoes of all sizes and shapes that a boat could possibly take, and wonderfully made paddles. The place was also full of face masks hideous in both shapes and colours. Here the neighbouring tribes no doubt met, and held their dances and potlatches, ceremonies too well known now to be described here.

Many evenings were spent by McKenzie and the *Tilikum* crew at the Beal Lighthouse where every hospitality was shown by the keeper,[9] his wife, and their children. This job of lighthouse keeper always struck me as being one that should go down in books of fame for it was one far more lonesome than a trip across the Pacific in a canoe. Even though the lighthouse keepers at Beal were sure of good wholesome new food, they commanded a cow, chickens, and fish and game the year round for the taking.

One morning I got up early just as the day was breaking. I could not believe my eyesight and was sure it was a mirage. No one was in sight at either of the villages so I could not ask for corroboration, but there it was, if my eyes told the truth, a great big four mast square-rig merchantman. How it ever got under Cape Beal Lighthouse and into Alberni Inlet without being dashed to pieces on the rocks is a mystery to this day to every sailor on the coast. Running down to the beach and pushing out my canoe, I was soon paddling to the ship. Long before I got alongside I was being talked to, howled at would be better, by one of the most excited German sailing masters I had ever met. In very broken English this captain wanted to know where he was.

---

[9]   Department of Marine and Fisheries, *Annual Report*, 1901, Part II, Sessional Paper No. 21, p. 153. See "Statement Giving Names and Stations of Light-keepers." Thomas Patterson was the keeper of the Cape Beal Light, his date of appointment being given as March 2, 1895.

On being told he said I was a liar, and that Beal Light must be Flattery Light. A boat coming into the Strait of Juan de Fuca from the Pacific swings around Flattery Light. By some fluke of fortune this German captain missed the sailors' graveyard, as this west part of Vancouver Island is called, and made the only possible entrance for a boat of this size from the Pacific for miles along the coast, under Beal Light. He not only made a port that would require very careful work in fine weather, but made it in the worst storm the elements could compose. Beal Light was comparatively new, perhaps he had no chart of it. He next asked me if he could get a tug as he wanted to get-damn-Hell out of God water-quick fast. On being assured one could be notified at Victoria by wire from Beal Light, he threw five English sovereigns tied in a handkerchief into my canoe, with accompanying adjectives of English, German, and French. I paddled at once for Beal Light and reported the ship to the keeper who was not quite sure yet that the coming and going of that large German merchantman was not a dream. Returning to the German captain I told him that two tugs would arrive that day. Even then he would not believe me, but told me again that I was a liar and once more recited a whole volume of swear words. He told me if I was not a liar he would give me more gold, and he kept his word. He actually cried huge tears mixed up with most expressive language when he saw the first tug coming in. But when the second one came in sight he cried harder than ever and did his best to kiss me, but did not succeed. I promised him a good punching if he tried such expressions of feelings again.

All day long until the next day the German captain stayed in a state of insanity, again and again asking the tug captains to save his ship, promising them large rewards if they kept their word. It was several days before the weather moderated sufficiently for these staunch little giants of tugs that withstood any storm, risked taking the big ship to Victoria. The visit of all these boats livened the *Tilikum*'s stay considerably, and it was the firm conviction of both tug captains and crews that the *Tilikum* would never reach its journey's end, such was the delightful discussion I heard one day between the captains of the tugs. I had the ten sovereigns in my pocket at the time, and promptly approaching the captains I offered to bet my handful of gold that the *Tilikum* would make the islands somewhere south of the equator. My bet, however, was not accepted. When asked by the captains why I was taking so mad a voyage I assured them that it was an undertaking purely and solely for adventure, to see the islands of the South Seas and to see them where and when I wanted. There was no foundation in the story the newspaper had that a wager of thousands of dollars had been made.[10] In fact, the bet just offered them was the first and only one I had ever made, and when they heard the *Tilikum* had successfully made Beal Light on the 27th from some sixty miles at sea they became wonderfully impressed because they knew of what calibre the weather was at that date. A special visit was made later by them to the *Tilikum* to read the canoe log.

Closely following the departure of the excitable German captain came one of the sealing schooners, the *Sadie Turpel*[11] from Victoria on her way to Bering Sea, which had called in at Village Islands to recruit the seal hunters. The schooner was about five hundred tons with a crew of four or five whites and would take perhaps twenty

---

[10] "There was no money, wager or otherwise, involved in the *Tilikum* trip as Voss wrote in his book," Luxton wrote elsewhere.

[11] Department of Marine and Fisheries, *Annual Report*, 1901, Part II, Sessional Paper No. 21b, p. 307. See "List of Shipping . . . on the Registry Books of the Dominion of Canada on the 31st day of December, 1901." *Sadie Turpel*: port of registry, Victoria; owner or managing owner, Victoria Sealing Co., Ltd., Victoria. See also *Daily Colonist* (Victoria, B.C.), October 30, 1901, which reports the return to Victoria of the *Sadie Turpel*, Captain John Bishop, "with 199 skins." See also, *Captain's Ledger, Sadie Turpel*, 1901.

Indian hunters. It took the best part of a week before the deal was made with the hunters and then another week before the Indians got through making their medicine and getting ready.

It was just before this schooner sailed that I almost lost my trip in the *Tilikum*. On board this sealing schooner was my chum and roommate of Victoria days and schoolchum of youthful days, Mr. Henry Copeland[12] of Winnipeg, Manitoba. He, it seemed, knew the *Tilikum* had been storm bound at Indian Village, and had with Ollie B. Ormond,[13] the third chum of the trio, also of Victoria and Winnipeg, made it up that Cope would go to Indian Village and by fair means or foul compel me to give up such a mad, fool idea of a trip across the Pacific in a canoe. First he tried sympathy, love, family, mother, until we almost fought, when Cope apparently gave up the job, and for days the subject was discussed no more. The night before the schooner sailed Cope asked me to dinner on it. Cope was more of a guest to the schooner captain than one of the crew, so I, all innocent of vile intent, was forcibly locked up in one of the cabins of the schooner that night after dinner. Shanghaied in fact, and to Bering Sea, Cope had made up his mind he would go. It was not

---

[12] Letter from Mrs. S. J. Vale (daughter of Henry Copeland), Winnipeg, Manitoba, March 9, 1969. Henry W. D. Copeland was the son of William Cook Copeland, who was Chief Clerk of the County in Winnipeg. Henry was born in St. Catharines, Ontario, in 1876, and went to school in Winnipeg, later becoming Deputy Clerk of the County. He served in the Armed Forces from 1914–18. He had two sons and two daughters. He died in 1944 in Deer Lodge Military Hospital, Winnipeg.

[13] See *Daily Colonist* (Victoria, B.C.), October 23, 1960, obituary. Oliver Blair Ormond was born in Peterborough, Ontario, on March 19, 1871. He was a resident of Victoria for 65 years. In 1898, he was listed as operating a book and stationery store. He farmed in Gordon Head with a brother, serving a term on the Saanich Council. Later he became secretary and director of Ormond's Ltd., a local biscuit manufacturing firm. He died on October 1, 1960.

until well after two o'clock in the morning that I removed a panel from the door with a huge clasp knife I carried. No one heard me leave the vessel, and not until the morning was my escape discovered. Cope even then was not licked. Getting two of the schooner's crew he started to row across to the *Tilikum* the hundred yards or so that I swam that morning, but on being greeted with a loaded sixteen bore shotgun the rowers decided it was no place for them and in spite of Cope's protests and offers of bribery, they returned to the sealing schooner which shortly raised her anchor. And the *Sadie Turpel*, dipping her flag, sailed away to a most successful hunt.

Once more I took to hunting for the island was a real paradise for collectors. This inlet was studded with small islands covered with trees, full of material for a taxidermist, the bays and coves with all kinds of water-fowl and fish, so that with McKenzie's wonderful cooking the table never lacked for the best of food, and I collected many scientific specimens which I shipped back home before leaving Vancouver Island.

Before the *Tilikum* left Victoria, the crew drew up partnership papers, the legal firm of Langley and Martin[14] of Victoria doing the work. Captain Voss was senior officer, I first mate,[15] and I reserved all

---

[14] E. O. Scholefield and S. W. Howay, *British Columbia from the Earliest Days to the Present* (Vancouver, B.C.: S. J. Clarke Publishing Company, 1914), IV, 795-60. "Langley and Martin, lawyers. Old and well-known firm headed by William Henry Langley, who was born in 1868 in Victoria. For two years, 1901 and 1902, he was a partner with Archer Martin, later the Honourable Chief Justice Martin, born in Hamilton, Ontario, 1865. From 1903–06, Alexis Martin, brother of Archer, was Langley's partner." See also C. W. Parker, ed., *Who's Who in Western Canada*, (Vancouver, B.C.: Canadian Press Association, 1911), I, 258–59.

[15] Voss stated in his book Luxton had never been at sea but Luxton writes elsewhere, "I held first mate papers. I had qualified under Captain Anderson of the sealing fleet to Bering Sea in 1898–99 and 1900, so Voss is a liar again."

literary rights of the adventure. The *Tilikum* was to be used in any manner whatsoever, to make money, show purposes, particularly in civilized ports. If either partner quit, through sickness or otherwise, he sacrificed one-third of his half interest. It was a simple, cut and dried agreement. Captain Voss could not order the canoe to wherever he wished, though senior officer. I really was the business manager, and in like manner had to consult Voss as he had to consult me as to places to sail. So when I decided to go black fish or whale hunting with my Indian friend of the boils, I was somewhat surprised when Captain Voss decided to sail from Vancouver Island that very day. Voss was always a little afraid of losing his sailing mate, and his action in opposing the whale hunt I attributed to that reason.[16] At any rate, the whale hunt came off and lasted two full nights and a day and a half. By this time the storms had abated and the weather was ideal.

Two large canoes took to the ocean, six paddlers in one and eight in the other, with a headman and harpooner in each, I being one of the eight paddlers. Sailing west, these open dugout canoes, with no centre board or keel and only one big sail pretty well fore, easily made eight miles an hour. The first day out nothing was seen that could be overtaken. Some thirty or forty miles from Vancouver Island everyone dozed sitting or lying down rolled in a blanket. The weather was perfect, with only the Pacific roll and a gentle breeze. At about ten o'clock the second day out a school of whale or black fish was sighted, scattered along as far as the eye could see, and all heading north toward the island.

It was not long before the two canoes were right in the midst of the migration. The sail and mast were stowed and paddles were used to supply power. Every man was bare to the waist, and the striker in

---

[16] "Voss did not go on the whale hunt [as he claims in his book]. I went and was gone several days—Voss raised hell because he was afraid I might not come back," N. K. Luxton wrote elsewhere.

the bow of the canoe held ready in his hand a beautiful harpoon on the head of the throwing shaft. The harpoons were made by the Indians, the actual blade of metal being some four inches wide, and fitted to a short shaft which was inserted in the end of the throwing shaft. It was all bound with sinew string and glutted together with beeswax and resin. It was not much more than six inches long and was naturally a terribly wicked weapon in a skilled hand, and readily sank two feet or more into the body of a whale, and even further if the arm was strong and skilled in throwing it.

Almost at once when the canoes got into the school of fish a whale came within striking distance of the smaller canoe. Quick as a flash the striker had sunk his first harpoon. To the thong was tied a huge bladder, generally taken from a sea lion or a large short-haired seal, the throwing shaft coming free when the whale sounded. But neither canoe could get within striking distance again before the paddlers became winded, and the whale disappeared, harpoon, bladder, and all. Then Mr. Indian of the boils took command, and his strategy was good as a paddler interpreted the Siwash to me. The canoe that made the strike would paddle after the whale, and the other canoe would rest, paddling easily. When the first canoe paddlers became winded the second canoe could take up the chase in earnest. In this manner of attack the whale would be kept in sight. Fifteen or twenty minutes were consumed to explain this, and by that time the paddlers were all fresh again.

Once more the canoes spread sail and headed well for the island, the direction the fish were going. It was past noon when the small canoe got another throw. A huge black fish came up within ten feet of the canoe, and put consternation into the paddlers with its closeness. In went the harpoon, and before the whale sounded another blade with bladder attached was registered. In a few minutes the whale, instead of coming up somewhere in a straight line to the direction it was going, came to the surface close to my canoe. Apparently the first harpoon had done some vital harm because the canoe had no difficulty getting close enough for the third harpoon to be sunk home. To this harpoon was attached a long slender line, and it was a marvel how the striker hung fast to it, only letting out what the whale demanded when he went down, the paddles going faster now than ever before.

Once, while on the surface, the whale took the canoe for a ride I will never forget. We went so fast the canoe rocked until it was all but ready to turn over and spin. While four or five of the crew balanced the canoe the others bailed and bailed barrels of water. The rest of the crew kept on balancing while the striker watched the line and manipulated it around a post purposely fastened in the canoe for such an occasion. For thirty minutes or more the whale kept going, and the companion canoe was soon lost to sight. Suddenly, the whale sounded again, this time going so deep that nearly all the line was run out. When it finally did stop the line was retrieved by paddling quickly. The whale was failing fast, and in a few minutes the canoe came within twenty feet and three more blades with bladders were sunk into its sides, spurring the whale into racehorse speed for a few moments more. Once again the harpoons registered, and this was repeated several times until the whale's whole back was covered with twenty or more bladders, these bladders having been inflated during the heat of the whale's races.

All this time I was conscious of the striker in the bow and the headman in the stern of the canoe carrying on a continuous conversation, but both talking at once. Finally, I asked the paddler next to me what they were talking about, and in a low whisper the Indian informed me that they were talking to the whale, telling him what a very fine whale he was, and that if he kept on swimming in the direction he was going they, the Indians, would take him into Dodge Cove and cure him of all his bad wounds. He could then return to his family and tell them what good people the Indians were. This talk actually went on for at least two hours, and finally the poor old black fish died.

The other canoe fastened many more bladders into him so that he would not sink. Then, and all that night, the canoes towed him toward Vancouver Island, landing there early the next morning some ten miles west of Beal Light. At high tide the whale was beached, and hardly before its back was well out of the water fifty or more Indians were at it with knives, saws, and axes. They cut it to pieces before the day was out. Pile upon pile of blubber was spread along the beach. Many "hatches" were cut into it from its "deck," and in and out of these holes climbed long-haired, greasy women, handing out large strips of meat and blubber. Everyone was cooking and eating it, and hundreds of pounds were consumed that day. Then it was divided into piles, with each family getting a share according to their numbers. Small amounts of money and many presents were heaped on the two successful canoes that had made the kill. It was a wonderfully exciting experience, and one of the best I had on the entire trip.[17]

---

[17] The late Dr. Clifford Carl, Curator of the British Columbia Provincial Museum, was of the opinion that this was the last great whale hunt by coast Indians.

IV

At Sea

The Tilikum *gets to sea, miles of whales cause
consternation. Something to do about a whale and
killer whales. Also sea anchor and currents.*

It was with real regret that on July 6th the *Tilikum* bade farewell to dear old Mr. McKenzie and many Indian friends. The anchor was raised and made fast to the top of the foredeck, and by nine o'clock the canoe was away from the coast, leaving from Vancouver Island through a fair weather passage out to Alberni Inlet several miles west of Beal Light. Captain Voss set a course south, bearing east with a strong west wind. It was our intention to try to make that very famous island, Pitcairn, renowned for the hiding there of the crew of the *Bounty*, which was not reported as found until twenty-five years after. Why Voss and I picked this island as our southern boundary goodness only knows. Perhaps it was the glamour it possessed, as the mutineers of the *Bounty* hid there. Also, a call at the Marquesas Islands was looked forward to with interest, or any other islands that happened on the horizon. We intended to cross the equator at about one hundred and twenty-five degrees west longitude. At any rate, Pitcairn was never reached by the *Tilikum*, but right away the adventure started. It was some twenty-five miles away from Beal Light when the *Tilikum* ran into miles of whales, yes it was miles of whales, and if the Siwash whale hunters had been there they would have found no trouble in spearing a whale every five minutes.

It was along towards my watch when Voss let a yell out of him, and I could feel the boat from where I was in the cabin turn sharply off her course to prevent hitting a sleeping whale, I afterwards discovered from Voss. All night long, from midnight until six a.m. I kept an oar balanced as a teeter, hitting the cabin deck to scare the whales away. Dozens of times I got the spray blown into my face from a spouting whale and a more offensive odour I have never had in my nose. It was far from a pleasant feeling sitting there in the dark and hearing that peculiar goo or goff. It sounded more like a deep note echoing in a well, rolling into you and all around you from the dark, that the whale makes when he comes to the surface to breathe. It was the first afternoon out from Vancouver Island that Voss again let a yell out of him to come on deck. I had just finished washing the breakfast dishes and was dozing off into the first sleep when Voss's voice brought me up through the cabin hatch in a hurry. Away off over our port bow we could see a whale and to all appearance he was playing in a very turbulent manner, or he was in trouble and travelling very fast, parallelling our course in the opposite way. Voss said at once that sharks were tackling the whale. This was a new one to me and I certainly watched every move of the fight. It might have lasted five minutes or an hour, it seemed easily ten or fifteen minutes now that I can look back to it. There was a chap by the name of F. St. Mars, who wrote a story of these fighting fish and a whale for the *Adventure* magazine some time in 1926. I often wonder if Voss had by any chance ever told him what he saw that day. His story is not embellished an item, and if he had been there he could not have told what we saw more perfectly. The whale kept jumping half out of the water as the killers sprang clean out of the water, falling to strike the whale with their tails, which looked to me like Turkish swords. In and out of the water they flashed, each time dealing the whale a blow that cut many inches long and deep. The ocean was turned into a millpond of foam and bubbles and fat, and the roll of the Pacific was actually flattened out as by that time the whale had slowed down. All the arena lacked were the posts and the ropes, the roll of the Pacific was the bleachers, and the *Tilikum* the reserved seats. Such a fight! It is beyond description. The thresher sharks never seemed to pause, each time falling back into the water, after their sword sweeping cuts, with a smack that we heard long before the fight was within detail sight. I really felt sorry for the whale. Try as he might, he never once hit a thresher with the flukes of his tail that whirled and thrashed around so fast and quick I wondered that such a huge mammal could show such agility. Twice the poor old beggar disappeared only to come to the surface again head first and always with the thresher after him. Suddenly everything disappeared, as our arena was being blotted out by the roll of the ocean. The crimson brown of the water was assuming its natural blue, and Voss was getting the canoe before the wind. We had hauled to in order to watch the fight. Voss was trying to tell me about these thresher sharks. I was standing with my elbows on the top of the cabin roof, and my feet on the floor of the cabin, when right out of the water came that damned whale, head first not ten feet from our canoe, and so placed that I would be right in the middle of his fall when he fell. Now I had seen him in this position several times in the past fifteen minutes, and each time he fell keel down. I think I tried to loosen one of the oars tied along the outside cabin wall, yelling at Voss to get under way. I had an insane idea of pushing the canoe out of the way of the whale or pushing the whale away from the canoe, when bang, at the height of my excitement that very accommodating and much abused whale fell over backwards with a report that sounded like a snow slide hitting green timber in the Rocky Mountains. The very tip end of one of the flukes of his tail as it came out of the water hit the batten that held down the canvas which covered the *Tilikum's* deck, and ripped it off, as you might flip a tooth pick from your thumb and finger. When the whale was in the air, standing on his tail as it were, it looked to me a terrible thing. Certainly, he must have been fifteen feet above us. I could see his body tapering to the tail and his poor belly was one mass of holes that could plainly be seen, the fat and blubber bulging out like a cut skin of putty. These holes were caused by that most abominable of all creatures the swordfish, which had kept the whale on the surface of the ocean while the killers did the work, murder. Murder it must have been for we never saw the whale again. What a feast the creatures of the deep had you can only know by reading F. St. Mars's article.

Well, I looked at Voss and I thought he must have become seasick for of all the deadly pale looking sailors he was the limit, and when I lifted my arms from the cabin roof I'll be hanged if I didn't flop. My knees refused to support me. Voss was quite as frightened as I was. I crawled to the bunk where it was some time before my nerves let me alone, and I could sleep. That same evening when I took my watch at the tiller about seven o'clock we passed through a number of very large sea lions,[18] but they looked quite gentle and lamb-like, compared to what we had witnessed that afternoon.

The next morning, July 7th, our second day out, I cooked breakfast of oatmeal, toast and coffee, with sugar and canned cream, and passed Jack out his share. This was the procedure that all during the trip we adhered to. The man coming on watch cooked the meal. All day long the north wind held steady, and the little boat reeled the

---

[18] A kind of large-eared seal, often with a mane, found in the Pacific Ocean.

miles off like a regular ship. Jack tried the *Tilikum* sailing wing and wing, the mainsail pulling from the port side and the foresail from the starboard, and the jib and spanker sails reversed, but the canoe rocked so badly that after an hour of it we were both glad to change the sails all to the port side. In this position and with a steady wind the canoe was as easy riding as any sailing boat I was ever in. My experience at sea was of course limited compared to Voss's. A time or two around Vancouver Island, with many short trips, and two trips into Bering Sea, were all I had ever had in sailing boats. But on a trip by canoe in the Rocky Mountains from the head waters of the Athabasca River in British Columbia to Lake Ontario I had covered thousands of river and lake miles, and no doubt this experience stood me in good cause.

I have seen seas on Lake Manitoba and Lake Winnipeg from a York boat[19] such that Voss would have very quickly hove to. In fact, there were very few of the old Hudson's Bay Company's fur water routes, that they had followed for years before the railways came in that I had not been over. "Heaving to," is putting your bow into the face of the storm, hoisting up some kind of stern-sail, pulling the

---

[19] *Encyclopedia Canadiana*, 1965, X, 392–93. "York boat: first built at York Factory on Hudson Bay by the Hudson's Bay Company, hence name. Most usual length and width forty feet by ten feet amidships. Heavy keels, stout posts at stem and stern, close ribs, thick planking and flat bottoms because designed to be dragged or rolled on logs across rough portages partly loaded. Pointed at both ends and sides sloped inwards. Heavy wooden rudder was hung astern in some craft, or a long oar for steering. Crew eight to fifteen depending on size of boat or nature of waterway. Boat rowed by oars called 'sweeps' sometimes fourteen feet long, which pivoted on stout upright wooden pegs set into the gunwales. Speed six knots in quiet water. A long mast, braced with ropes was slung against the outside of one of the gunwales. When wind favourable, a canvas sail, shaped like a truncated pyramid, was hoisted. The top was spread by a free swinging yard arm, and the bottom usually wider than the boat, was secured to the mast guy ropes. The sail bellied out much as a spinnaker."

sheet in tight, and making a riding-sail. Thus if the boat swings sideways to the wind she will not get very far before she is blown back with her bow facing into the teeth of the gale. It helps the bow stay in that position to drop an anchor over the bow, be it a bag of stone or a regular anchor. Often have I seen the Indians do this very thing in very small canoes, and ride out a gale in safety.

Voss's ideas were very much more scientific in weathering a storm, and the fact that Voss sailed across all the largest oceans in the world in the *Tilikum*, except the North Atlantic, is proof positive that he knew his business, and he learned it by going easy. I only once ever saw Voss take a chance. He never gave a storm any benefit of any doubt, and he never sailed until he even lost a sheet, always anticipating trouble. Many's the Hell he has given me for not taking in sail when perhaps I should have. Voss, I think, could have sailed around the world with one sight for position every ten days, and he could guess his position by dead-reckoning and never be wrong more than five miles in a twenty-four hour run, all that regardless of wind or currents. Generally speaking, Voss was a kind-hearted man but sometimes he would have black moods and then he was all a man should never be. The little newspaperman[20] that went with Voss on a treasure hunt on Cocos Island, pleaded with me more than once not to sail with Voss. He said he would likely kill me, claiming that his body was sore for days through the beating that Voss and his mate had inflicted on him during that voyage. Voss was not what any person would term a daredevil or even a fearless man. At his best he was quite methodical and sure of himself, always, before he acted. When roused and in his black moods it took a lot to stop him. Neither could he handle liquor, so that outside of a few ounces that I carried in the medicine chest, no spirits of any kind went into the stores of the *Tilikum*.

---

[20] This was the man, Mac, referred to in Voss's voyage to Cocos Island in the *Xora*. Luxton refers to him elsewhere but always just as Mac.

Voss had often told me how he would heave to in a storm and for days work on what he called a "sea anchor," that would minimize the drift to a boat when hove to, and could in many ways be used to advantage. He got the idea from an old sailor in the North Sea, and that it was a good one has been proven time and again by many sailors. One of Voss's sea anchors, we used it on all our trip, was a wooden barrel hoop about twenty inches in diameter, with a four foot cone-shaped canvas bag sewed to the hoop. At the point or small end of the bag a hole of about three to four inches was made and carefully bound so that the water would not fray or unravel the canvas. To one side was fastened a small weight to keep the hoop perpendicular in the water, and to the same hoop were fastened three ropes which in turn were fastened to the end of the cable that held it to the boat. This cable was then let out until it rode about half-way or better between each wave. That is, if the boat hove to and was on the crest of a wave, the sea anchor would be half-way to the next wave. Once, for seventeen days the *Tilikum* rode to such an appliance and a drag, and never shipped a cup of water. The weather was composed of samples of everything that misnamed Pacific could put up.

The drag is most important. It might be a bundle of blankets, a piece of furniture, anything about the size of a sack. This is tied by its own line to the bow of the boat and floats to the crest of the oncoming wave that would sweep the deck of the boat. Meeting this small resistance of the drag the crest of the wave is broken, thus making a canyon for the boat to pass through. The line of the drag should be played out far enough so that when the boat is on the crest of a wave the drag would be on the crest of the next oncoming wave, while the sea anchor line is only out half the distance. The sea anchor keeps the boat head on, and the drag breaks the white waters or top of the wave which otherwise would sweep the boat and break it into kindling wood.

In *The Venturesome Voyages of Captain Voss*, he appendixed to his story some twenty paragraphs of advice, and I know that if Voss had not followed them himself we would never have reached our first island. For this advice he gives to the world, if for nothing else, I could readily forgive Voss for breaking his agreement with me by stealing the *Tilikum*'s story across the Pacific, for he has given to the seafaring men foolproof advice which if followed out will save many ships and more lives.

Voss's observations on the 9th showed the boat to be two hundred and thirty-nine miles from Beal Light, and one hundred miles from the American coast. All that day the *Tilikum* was running into and crossing rip tides, some a few hundred feet wide and some wider. The noises of the rip, rip, rip of these streams could be quite distinctly heard above the other ocean noises, and as the bow of the canoe launched into them there was often an appreciable side swing to the canoe as it entered the current. The water in this vicinity carried a different colour and surface and there was also quite a difference in the temperature[21] of the rip tide and the ocean water.

---

[21] Luxton must have been mistaken. Hydrographic sources in Victoria have assured the editor that a rip tide has no effect upon water temperature.

V

The Doldrums

Sperm whales inspect the Tilikum. Three hundred fifty miles from Vancouver Island is sighted the first vessel. Sea anchor in use for first time. Sight the second and last ship on the entire trip. Gooneys great company. Shark drives me back to the canoe. A swordfish gets his breakfast. Wonderful light effects. Doldrums a wonder-world. Electric storms appalling. Thirty-six hour blow.

This morning of July 10 I wakened up to the fact that we had a cricket on board, and to hear him you would think he was trying to act for the canary that we did not include in our manifests. He was a cheerful fellow and stayed with us until we landed on the first island. Often at nights, when sleep seemed to desert us, his bright sharp clicking broke the monotony of the water noises. Today our sight tells us we travelled ninety-six miles, three hundred thirty-five miles from home, and we ran into another school of whales. They are all around us, black fish only, but large enough to raise trouble if they so much as grazed our hull. At seven I went on my watch. The whales were all gone, but I saw a strange looking object that looked like a grey rock, quite a mile off our port quarters. I called Voss out of the bunk and he pronounced it a sperm whale. Why, these black fish were only pups alongside of this old cow whale as she proved to be, because suddenly, away from behind her came her calf. The darned little fool sighted the *Tilikum* and he came to see what we were. Take it from me, I was not at all anxious for any close company of baby whales with a mother whale kicking around as big as a C.P.R. Empress. He came within a hundred and fifty feet, stopped, and looked us over. I asked Jack to make a noise like a shark but he only looked at me sort of serious and did not say anything. That whale was only a baby certainly. I don't suppose he was hungry but he might take a fancy to our white canoe and take a bite out of it, or he might want to come and play with it. Anyway, he sized us up good and plenty, a more deliberate thinkable stare at the *Tilikum* was never less appreciated by both the crew. Then he turned around and when mamma saw him coming back she changed her course too, and both headed the way all whales we met those days were going. About twelve o'clock that night it started to blow. In order to sustain balance I had to brace my feet on the opposite side of the cockpit, and hang on to the tiller with both hands. I called Jack for his watch at one a.m. and in about an hour it was blowing from the north-northwest so fresh that Jack took in the spanker and the mainsail. I got very little sleep that night and at nine a.m. the canoe was travelling the fastest she had ever gone under foresail and jib only. At ten a.m. over our stern we sighted the first vessel we had seen, and at eleven-thirty a.m. she passed us. She proved to be the three masted schooner *Excelsior*,[22] from Vancouver,

---

[22] *Lloyd's Register of British and Foreign Shipping*, I (1901) and II (1902–03). "*Excelsior*, wood three-masted schooner; 331 tons; owner: D. Steffens, 44 East Street, San Francisco; port of registration, San Francisco."

loaded with lumber. We did not speak to her but I got some snap-shots of her with the camera. We could see the crew watching us through glasses, and darned if it wasn't lonesome after she dropped below the horizon. Our old relic must have felt her hundred years of service and the heavy seas were working the natural cracks of her hull, for I had to get busy with the bailer and bail water out of the well which was just fore of the water tanks and about five inches deep. At three p.m. the waves got to be breaking waves so Jack hove the *Tilikum* to,[23] with the sea anchor and a drag as well. Our hol-lowed log of wood, lying about three points off the wind, was as dry if not so comfortable as if she had been in Dodge Cove. All afternoon and all that night we went up and down more hills of water in the shape of waves than there are mountains in British Columbia. It was rough riding, and got very tiresome, one of us always in the cockpit and the other in the bunk. About ten a.m. Voss sang out to pull in the drag and sea anchor.[24] I guess he could not stand it any longer and we ran before the wind under trysail or jib only. The *Tilikum* flopped and kept on flopping and pitching until she got a reefed foresail on her, then she steadied down to that uphill, half over and bang as she rode each wave. That day I cooked two sets of breakfasts as the first

---

[23] Voss, in speaking of this incident, gives Luxton a lecture on breaking seas, to which Luxton writes: "Any d . . . fool who has been to sea would know this. Voss did not have to tell me." Voss says he ordered Luxton to put out the anchor, and though he had a life line around Luxton he climbed the foremast instead of dropping anchor, to which Luxton wrote: "Voss apparently tells this supposed story of me to illustrate what might have happened. Certainly none of it did. Anyhow even the mainmast was too small for a very small man to climb."

[24] Here Voss says in his book that he took down the storm-sail, took in the sea anchor and hoisted the staysail, to which Luxton wrote: "It took both men always to get the boat away again after being under drag. One man to haul in the sea anchor and drag and the other to hoist the staysail or jib and swing the boat between the waves."

rolled off the stove. Jack said he never knew I was a poet. One thing about Jack Voss was that he seldom if ever swore. He was not a fluent English speaker, but he never showed his lack of adjectives by using cuss words. That day one of the water tanks sprang a leak, but I managed to get it stopped with a little flour dough.

On that day, the 13th, at four p.m. the wind had gone down quite a lot and all sail was put on the canoe. That same day Voss got a sight at noon which put us one hundred and eight miles in twenty-one hours from where we had been hove to the day before. This was good travelling under less than half her sails.

On Sunday the 14th I felt just as if I was missing church and should be on my way. Jack was on watch that morning. There was a good stiff blow and Voss was still experimenting with the sails. He was nothing if he was not a student of boats and sails. I was puttering around the cabin locker, sorting out "swollen heads" among our canned goods, when Jack called for me to come up and see a ship. He altered our course south by west to southeast in order that we might cross her course, and it was only a few moments later that we ran under her stern. She was the *Mary Winkelman*,[25] from Honolulu to San Francisco, loaded with sugar. We just had time to get the captain's reading or sight of longitude of the day before, which was 129° 11', compare chronometers, ask him to report us, and we were past speaking range. The captain's lady, who was hanging over the bulwark with the crew, asked me if I had permission to leave home, this in the short while that the captain was rushing away to get the time,

---

[25] "Voss here is an awful liar [in his book], it was the day after the storm we passed the boat. We only had two or three minutes—moving all the time. The barquentine had suffered in a storm if I remember, most of her sails were gone, and one mast broken off," N. K. Luxton wrote elsewhere. *Lloyd's Register of British and Foreign Shipping*, I (1901). "*Mary Winkelman*, wood bark; 482 tons; owner: Charles Nelson and Co., 6 California Street, San Francisco; port of registration, San Francisco."

and she did her best to get us on board. But there was a pretty good sea, so why take the chance of breaking our canoe. They reported us on their arrival at San Francisco. I saw the paper after, and I will bet anything that the *Tilikum* got a circulation of several million readers the following twenty-four hours after the newspaper boys turned out. My father, who was an M.P.P.[26] the best part of his life, said he had never had anything like the publicity we got that following week.

It was some comfort to speak to this ship because it proved that our Waltham chronometer was keeping wonderful time, outside of losing one-fifth of a second every twenty-four hours. Also, through meeting the *Mary* which I next saw in Newcastle, Australia, I won a bet from a chap of that city. He was optimistic enough to back his opinion that the *Tilikum* had not crossed the Pacific. A short walk from the pub, where the bet was laid, to the *Mary Winkelman*'s deck, proved to my sceptical friend's satisfaction, that he was a loser.

I never liked passing ships at sea. It always upset our domestic calm, and economic conditions were all disorganized. The old cricket was the only one of the crew that seemed more cheerful, no matter what happened, so right after speaking to the *Mary* I got busy on the fore hatch. Here was where the bulk of our provisions were stored, and it was a pitiful sight. We had been out of Village Islands only eight days, seven hundred and twenty-five miles from Vancouver

---

[26] W. F. Luxton was elected to the second Legislative Assembly of the Province of Manitoba for the Rockwood Constituency December 23, 1874, and sat until 1878. He resigned to contest the Marquette Constituency for a federal seat; however, he and Joseph O'Connell Ryan retired to allow Sir John A. Macdonald to be elected by acclamation. On the 9th of December, 1886, W. F. Luxton was elected to the sixth Legislative Assembly of Manitoba as a member for South Winnipeg and sat until the general election of July 11, 1888. *List of General Elections and of Members Elected*, manuscript handbook compiled by Charland Prud'homme, Chief Electoral Officer of the Province of Manitoba.

(counting in twenty-four hours hove to), and green mould was everywhere. Our suit-cases were as green as Christmas trees. Boxes of sea biscuits were pushing the nails out of the boxes, wrappers on the tins were all coming off, and there was more water there than in the cabin. It was not long before I had the water tight bulwark with the chinking out of it, and the water draining back to where it could be bailed out. What provisions had suffered worst I removed to the cabin until we could only get into our bunks by crawling across the stove. This green mould was a nuisance throughout the whole trip. It ruined clothes, spoiled our grub, and made me very ill. It was so bad that I had to pick over our oatmeal flake by flake, all according to colour. It was the whites against the greens, the latter always winning by ten to one. Then we would go "gow" all day after eating it. A teaspoon of soda would relieve the pressure at our pants' bands, but it was uncomfortable and sickening so I only made enough for Voss and drank coffee for breakfast. I got out a fresh plug of T. and B. smoking. It was quite as thick as three plugs should be and so damp that it bent like rubber. We cut it up and dried it in the sun on deck, but a lot of its flavour was lost.

At twelve midnight, on July 15th, it was one of the most perfect of all space, stars, and water combinations that could be put together. An hour after it was breezing so hard that I was glad Voss came on watch to do what he liked with taking the sail. He kept it all on, sailing the *Tilikum* all day four and a half to five points on the wind. This was one of his student days. He was studying the combination of winds and sails. All afternoon I fooled around about the cabin and on the foredeck. The gooneys[27] were a great source of amusement to me. One got so that it would come right up to the side of the boat and accept food out of my hand. I taught him to do

---

[27] The black-footed albatross of Pacific waters, sooty-brown plumage with a wing spread of up to seven feet.

this by tying a piece of fat pork to a string and trailing it over the stern of the canoe. When he grabbed the pork I would haul him in on the end of the string. When close to the boat he would let go, and the pork would gently slide out of his mouth and throat. I would immediately throw him a piece without any string on it. In a day or so he would come up to the canoe following the string and fairly spit out the pork the string was tied to as he apparently knew he would get a piece he could keep. I got him in the cockpit one day, but he made such a mess of the boat in his excitement that I was glad when he flopped over the side. It was a great temptation to make scientific specimens out of these wonderful birds, but I gave up the idea after they became so tame. Jack thought it was because I was superstitious, for he had told me if I killed them a great disaster would overtake the boat. The gooneys had a good time as long as they stayed, which was for many days, and only quit us when we reached warmer latitudes.

At five p.m. that day the weather thickened. We had logged ninety miles the last twenty-four hours. The next day, the 16th, it was almost dead calm, with a heavy roll from the northwest, hardly a steering breeze. Jack was sound asleep all morning, and I sewed ballast bags. At noon I took our position, as 126° 18' longitude. This only gave us forty-five miles run in the past twenty-four hours, and all afternoon it remained dead calm. I wished I could sleep like Jack, and eat like him too. Mildew and mouldy grub seemed to agree with him, but I was getting lighter than I ever was in my life.

July 17th, my diary reads, very little winds, and logged only fifty miles since the night before. It was getting very warm, my neck was badly sunburned, but the backs of Jack's hands were covered with water blisters. They were so bad that I was afraid of infection and made him wrap them up in sweet oil. Voss was a persistent devil. He became seasick every storm, he sunburned terribly, his hands and feet would crack open with the salt water, yet he loved the sea more

than any man I have ever met, and he couldn't swim.[28] We would tie
the anchor rope to the stays of the mainmast, and hop overboard
with it. We had been doing this right along ever since we left
Vancouver Island, but this day I quit it, a pail and a towel being good
enough. I saw a fin off to one side of me when I was on the end of the
rope. It was cutting the water, and there was no mistaking what it
was. I did hand over hand on the rope pulling myself to the boat in
world's record-time. I did not say anything to Voss about it as I was
breaking some of my own rules by bathing during watch, and doing
so when no one else was on deck. Voss came up ready to drop over
with the rope, and in the meantime I got out the old forty-four
Winchester, and some newspaper. I asked Voss to go forward and
throw newspaper, bundled into balls, as far out on each side of the
canoe as he could, and see what would happen. He did as I wished
and I made a peach of a shot through the shark's head as he came
out of the water to grab the paper. At the same time other pieces of
paper disappeared. Voss decided our swimming days were over and
that the millpond was closed. He also decided that he had just
missed being food for the sharks. From that time on there was hardly
a day passed that I did not kill one or more sharks, their kind friends
and brothers always relieving the ocean of their dead bodies.

I was getting pretty hungry by this time and one day I noticed a
fish, following under the canoe, that Jack called a bonito.[29] It was a
huge fellow, a good, clean, sporting-looking fellow. I got out my whaling spear and shaft, and tied a good strong whip-cord to the spear
thong. I had no trouble in spotting the fish, and shot down the spear.

---

[28] In Voss's voyage in the *Xora* he says he swam but Luxton wrote, "Voss could not
swim a stroke. He all but drowned with a rope around him one day in the Pacific,
when he fell overboard."

[29] One of the various large mackerel-like fish in the Pacific and Atlantic, up to
thirty inches long.

The fish gave a kick and disappeared. It was two or three days before I noticed him again, and right behind his head was a white scar. If I had struck a little harder I would have cut his head off. This wise fish used the boat for a cover so that he could raid schools of flying fish[30] which we were running through. After that I left the bonito alone, for almost every morning as the sun was rising he was the means of making the flying fish leave the water. Often I would pull in the sheets of the mainsail, and the flying fish would hit the sail and fall on the deck of the cabin, giving me a real breakfast. But one day we lost the bonito. Both Voss and I happened to be on deck when several waves off to our starboard we saw a huge swordfish jumping out of wave after wave, and heading straight for our bow. I don't know whether Jack pushed the helm or not, but the swordfish came so close to our canoe that I grabbed the stays on the main mast to receive the shock. The only one receiving the shock was the bonito. The ocean is certainly a cruel place. You can start with the weakest and work up to the top, and the strongest will have everything less strong than he is in his belly, dog eat dog, from the pup to the mastiff.

July 18th, about two it started to breeze up, and it blew all day and all night, until the morning of the 19th. I lost the sheets on both main and foresail during my watch. I guess that was my unlucky day. The heavy roll upset hot coffee all over my foot, leaving a lovely water blister, and it bothered me more than I cared to admit. An extra heavy roll, with a cross roll and a light breeze, shook us all ways. On July 20th the Northeast Trades came. We had done one hundred miles the day before. Sunday, July 21st, we were just two months away from Oak Bay, and fifteen days out, half-way to the equator. Sight showed longitude 125° 38', latitude 26° 57'. My diary says, foot sore as Hell.

---

30 Fish of warm and temperate seas. Large pectoral fins enable it to fly through the air for a short distance.

July 22nd, 23rd and 24th, there was a steady north and northeast trade wind and the canoe was doing ninety to one hundred miles every day. It was latitude 23° 28' on the 23rd. For the past two days the sky had been covered with heavy clouds, frequent mists making strange colouring on the water, and tinting the whole atmosphere. The sun was just going down behind a heavy bank of dark clouds, capped with snow white billows that lay the entire horizon around, giving it very much the appearance of a great range of mountains, when suddenly the dark changed to a deep purple, from purple to blue, then red and so on to a dozen different shades and colours. All space around us, even our white sails and boat, took on those wonderful shadings, with all colours changing very fast. The water was most beautiful, catching the light effects from the sky, the small white-caps looking more like clusters of wonderful jewels. The effect was weird and actually got on our nerves, in spite of its splendour. To crown it all, the largest and most perfect rainbow we had ever seen in our lives formed in the heavens. Yes, every colour shade in the universe was there at once. Suddenly the sun sank, and as quickly as you could count to three, all things had gone and it was night.

On the 24th we passed the sun north of us. On the 25th, 26th, and the 27th it was too cloudy for observations. We were certain that this must be the Doldrums, or very close to that part of the ocean that every sailing ship dreads so much. While it was cloudy it was as hot as it could possibly be and if the sun came out for a minute it made you hop to stand on deck.

To go forward it was necessary to slush the decks down with pails of water. The heat was too much for me and I had just about quit eating altogether. Jack spread an awning over the cockpit, from mainmast to mizzenmast, and it certainly was a great relief. The canoe was leaking pretty badly, the hot weather drying it out, and we had to bail out about ten gallons of water every eight hours. She seemed to be leaking all along her sides. Missed entering my diary yesterday, got a little off my head, but my foot is easier today and I think it is on the turn for the better. This is the 29th.

It is August the 1st. There is no doubt about it, this is the Doldrums, almost any kind of weather you can think of is here. I turned in at seven p.m. and went to sleep to awaken to the most confounded row imaginable. I could not think what it was, Jack had pulled the hatch shut on the roof. I yelled to him through the other half of the hatch, which was open, asking him what was the matter but he could not hear me at the top of my voice. It was dark as dark. I crawled to the hatch to find that it was raining, if it could be called rain. Water was falling in bunches. Two, two-inch scupper holes could not drain the cockpit. I got out with a pail and bailed it out to keep it from coming through the cabin hatch. A pail standing on the cockpit seat, eleven inches deep, was filled in a few minutes. This cloudburst lasted an hour, and believe me, I enjoyed it. I was clean once more, the first time I had been clean since leaving Victoria. These rains are not general, the area they occupy is very small. Several times during our stay in the Doldrums, I would see these storms away off, or sometimes within a quarter of a mile. I chased them around by pulling the canoe with oars, but I could never catch them. We hit the Doldrums in latitude 11° and 12° and stayed in an area of about one hundred and twenty five miles for seventeen days. We blew, when we blew, any direction and every direction but most of the time we were calm, with the ocean rolling two ways, and often the clouds rolling three ways. With proper grub and enough water this part of the ocean would be a wonderful place. I don't think there is a spot just like it in all the world. The electrical storms were appalling, lightning was so close we felt that it was right in the boat; in fact, it did hit us once. It took hold of the wire cables which stayed the mainmast, and shot down these into the ocean. Voss was lying on the bunk, and had his back braced against the sides of the canoe. He must have been touching one of the bolt heads that held the brace for he got a shock. It knocked him semi-conscious, and he stayed in bed almost twenty-four hours. These electrical storms were not pleasant, but were wonderful to witness, and you could always smell something like sulphur when they were raging. I don't suppose any artist could commence to put on canvas the wonderful light effects I saw for almost twenty days, and could no more describe them than I could Heaven. Certainly the Doldrums is no place for a bad-tempered man, for an artist to go crazy in, yes! Every evening at sunset it was at its best. From pole to pole, and from east to west, rising from the horizon the height of an hour's sun, were clouds of the most delicate snow white, and banked underneath them were clouds of constantly changing shades. Like one huge panorama floating around the entire horizon, taking shapes and making pictures of all the animal kingdom, prehistoric and present; castles, houses, cities, villages, forever changing and remaking. Suddenly this fairyland was swept away—fast—approaching like a bad spirit swept up from nowhere came a huge black canopy of clouds. It dropped in bursts of water that obliterated everything from view.

August 8th my diary says, having not touched it for three days, such confounded weather would take the heart out of anything. Voss asked me for my Bible today, and I think I told him to go somewhere, where we would be shortly anyhow. In desperation we would grab any wind that would take us south. Twice we had shaped our course for Samoa, giving up the Marquesas idea altogether, only to get a seductive wind that set our course southeast again, when a real wind suddenly came from the south that put the *Tilikum* under drag and sea anchor. This storm came up fast, sneaking up to us behind the pretty clouds. I was in the forehold to find where the canoe was leaking, when Jack started to yell for a drag and sea anchor. The goat blanket with some of the skulls tied in it that I had taken from the dead Siwash's canoe, was right at my feet, all tied up, and never thinking the waves would pound it all back to short hair with the sea anchor, I heaved both overboard. It made a dandy drag, and this storm was one of the worst we ever had on the entire voyage. That old goat blanket was a great resistance against the breaking waves. It simply tore the top off every one, leaving a road for the *Tilikum* to ride through. This gale kept up for almost thirty-six hours, with waves quite thirty-five feet high. It was one of the very few times I wished myself on land. It is a queer sensation to be thirty-five feet below a wall of water, that looks just as if it were going to fall right on top of you, when suddenly up goes the canoe and there is a roar of water on each side of you that you can't see over, with a path through the wall that the drag has made for the boat to go through. Then down once more you go into the trough of the next wave. Woe to you, if your cables on the drag or sea anchor slip or break. Just one little bit of those breaker waves need hit the fragile decks of the *Tilikum*, and everything would be kindling wood. It was during such storms and under drag that the watch had to have all his wits about him.

VI

Penrhyn Island

Why tell the truth and be a liar, a school of oil whales.
Something to eat at last, a turtle. Loss of fresh water.
Much bird life. The last of the Doldrums. A strange dream.
The canoe in the Southeast Trades breaks her own record.
Examine a derelict. Across the equator.
A porpoise gives adventure. Passing the first islands.
Running down Penrhyn Island.

I think it was when this worst of all storms was over, and when all was at its best, the atmosphere, horizon, sky-lines, and heavens shooting everything they had. Jack was below and I was sitting in the cockpit, swearing and cussing as usual. The canoe had just topped an unusually large wave and just as she was sliding out from under I happened to look off to the port side, and remarked to myself that that Doldrum animal was as near as real a one as I had yet seen. No matter if the canoe was in the trough or on top of a wave I could see this freak of nature, and I watched it for several minutes.

Suddenly I let a yell out of me, and that without even prompting myself, loud enough to bring Jack out of a sound sleep to the hatch. No one said a word, I silently pointed. To this day Jack has never spoken a dozen words about what we saw, though he did admit seeing the same thing once before. Jack never spoke about it because he said quite truthfully, no one would ever believe it, so why tell the truth and be a liar? You can believe it or not. According to Jack you won't and I don't care if you don't, but we both saw it and watched it for a good ten to fifteen minutes. How far away it was I haven't the slightest idea, perhaps a quarter of a mile or maybe a mile or two. There was nothing to judge distance by, and such a creature was not at all familiar. All kinds of whales we had seen and always felt we knew about how far away they were because we knew their size and could make comparisons, but this animal or mammal had never been classified in any natural history I had ever read. How far away it was or how high it was out of the water, how long it was, I could not say. It was moving along almost dead centre into the storm and apparently with no more effort than a whale had to move along with the waves. It was longer than any sailing ship I had ever seen, that I am sure of, and it stood out of the water higher than the waves that were then running, because its back lines were never awash. It did not appear to be at all stiff in the water like the body of a whale, it seemed to move at will, and carried its head, which was on the end of a huge neck, well out of the water. Fins or flukes we could not see, and its colours were all dark or greys. Out of the unknown it came like one of the storm's evil spirits, and into the darkest point of the stormy horizon it disappeared. Honestly, I never want to see another. Pink, blue and green elephants I have heard of under certain conditions, but if ever that un-nameable thing visited me in my dreams, I would cut Johnnie Walker cold, and all the rest of his Scotch friends.

It was August 10th that we got our first observation in five days, and we found we had made fourteen miles south in seven days and quite a lot west. Even in the Doldrums adventure followed the *Tilikum*. A large school of oil whales, Jack called them, passed us when we were under drag or hove to. They were not like the sperm whales and not as large, lighter in colour than the black fish of which we had seen so many. One passed quite close to the boat. He certainly looked great and magnificent in the raging storm. He was swinging with the waves on a perfectly even keel, and I would say going no faster than the waves. There he rode with the most graceful motions of anything I had ever seen at sea, riding along with the water and waves and slowing again as the wave broke and receded. Such rhythm in so huge and ungainly a mountain of flesh could never be understood if not seen. They were simply taking the road of least resistance, and somehow it struck me that they seemed to be enjoying it all, and knew perfectly what they were doing. Later, when the storm was abating I noticed what I could not mistake—a huge turtle. It was playing around the drag. Jack came on deck and took the whaling spear and shaft while I untied the rope from the anchor and tied it to the spear thong gradually pulling in the drag, the turtle coming right along with it. What he saw or smelled in that mess of torn and unravelled robe I have no idea. At any rate, he came so close to the canoe that handing the anchor rope, which was fastened to the thong of the spear, to Jack, and taking the shaft and spear from him, with one arm round the stays of the fore mast, I shot the spear as hard as I could through the centre of the turtle's back. It was a good thing that I had my arm on the stays, for the spear went clear through the turtle, and losing my balance, I fell off the deck into the water, but kept a hold on the stays and the spear shaft. Just when I was half-way back on deck, I saw Jack go overboard, and the last thing I saw of him, away down under the water were the soles of his feet. Jack hung on to the anchor line, and the turtle came back to the surface, so did Jack. By this time I had a hold too, and with a good perch for my feet against the stays of the mast, and sitting on the fore hatch, I soon pulled Jack on board. The turtle was not so easy. First of all he was not dead and secondly he was so big that he would not go into the canoe. It was several hours before we could hold him close alongside, and then I blew his head off with a forty-four bullet. This only seemed to liven him up for a while, but eventually he did die. I certainly would have liked to add him to my collection, but there was no place to put him, and after an amount of trouble we cut and hacked him to pieces with an axe and knife. If I could have kept the turtle fresh I would easily have reached normal weight again, but all too soon we had to feed him to the fishes. Even if most of it was wasted, it at least proved valuable while it lasted and broke the monotony of the Doldrums.

It was on August 11th that we commenced to think we were out of the Doldrums. We made thirty-eight miles south, and forty west, when it calmed down once more. Jack scraped the barnacles off the bottom of the boat while I listed it so he could see what he was doing. This made quite an improvement in our mileage.

It was Sunday and we always had pancakes. Jack was pretty strong on pancakes so he cooked them that day. Our bill of fare so far did not require a great deal of cooking and it was astonishing how well our wood was lasting. A few pieces the size of lead pencils boiled the water for coffee or porridge, or heated the canned meat and vegetables. Our menu ran like this: breakfast, oatmeal or corn meal, bread and coffee; lunch and dinner, canned tomatoes, peas or beans, ham or bacon, also canned meats and currie, bread and tea; at ten p.m. canned preserves, bread, tea or coffee. The bread, of course, was sea biscuits and everything that was not canned had green mould on it, and tasted accordingly.

Monday, August 12th, we discovered we had been bailing the fresh water out of the well that had been leaking out of our water tanks. One tank was all but empty and the other was only half full. This was not at all comforting and from then on we economized as much as possible with the water. No more seemed to be leaking out, the water was below the leak, which was somewhere that was impossible to get at. It was the fullest of the two tanks that leaked.

On August 13th a strong south by east wind, the first for days, came up. Birds were getting more numerous, and some I had never seen before. One, a boatswain[31] Voss called it, was pure white, with a strong head and back and the most gorgeous red feathers in his tail, which was from six to ten inches long, with a black quill. I found them in the islands later, but only in some places. The natives sneak up on these birds after dark, when the birds are roosting, and get hold of these long feathers pulling gently until the bird gets a good hold on the perch, then with a sharp pull relieve the bird of his two or three wonderful plumes. The islanders use them for decorations.

It seemed that about August 18th we were in for a real sailing breeze. We had been hove to for some eighteen hours. I was on watch and I think I must have been dozing. I woke up and the waves had died down considerably with the storm, but there was still white water. Sitting on the cabin roof, I suddenly saw my old friend George Grieve,[32] of Winnipeg, a dear and lovely old friend he had been to me through many years of my youth. To him I owed my love for collecting natural history specimens, for at the time he was one of the leading naturalists of the West. Quite plainly to my sleepy eyes I could see him, and while I cannot say that he told me in actual words to get busy and make sail, he told me to do just that, and to do it at once. I did not hesitate a moment to go forward, pull in the sea anchor and hoist everything the *Tilikum* had, and hit a course southwest. We had

---

[31] This is the boatswain or marlin-spike. Probably the reference is both to the skua-gull as well as the tropical bird.

[32] *Henderson's Directory: City of Winnipeg, 1900* (Winnipeg: Henderson Directories Ltd., 1901). "George Grieve, taxidermist; office, 247 Main Street; boarding, 334 Carlton Street, Winnipeg."

long ago decided to get out of these latitudes, even if we had to go back to Vancouver Island and start all over again. The even motion of the boat seemed to make Jack sleep sounder than usual after I got sail on, and it was daylight before he awoke. The *Tilikum* had been tearing it off for a good seven hours, and Jack was so glad to get out of the Doldrums that he forgot to give the usual Hell to me for hanging pants, shirts, towels or anything I could find to the stays and masts for extra sails. It was great to get going once more. There was a sequel to the appearance of my friend, George Grieve, in my dreams. I read in my Canadian papers when I got to Australia that he was dead, and had died shortly before he came and told me to make sail.

August 21st, my diary says, wind settled into steady Southeast Trades and we had been doing from one hundred to one hundred and seventy miles a day. Our observation put the canoe one and a half degrees north of the equator and one hundred and forty-one and a half longitude, one hundred and seventy miles, the best the canoe ever made, there must have been a strong current in our favour.

August the 22nd, I was once more in the fore hold and I had to throw the last box of sea biscuits overboard. It was a mass of green, stinking mould, and nearly all our canned goods, also rice and flour, oatmeal and corn meal followed. For five miles aft there was a line of floating food and thousands of gulls, man-of-war[33] and boatswain birds. The fish were after the food and the birds were after the fish. A gull gets a fish and the man-of-war birds chase him and make him drop it. He is a fine looking bird, but a terrible bully. Our water tanks were all but empty. I tried to get under several rain storms during my watch but had no luck. Unless we made Penrhyn Island soon, there were going to be two awfully thirsty men aboard the *Tilikum*. We were using tomatoes and peas for liquid refreshments, and we had

---

[33] Frigate bird, large bird of prey, hooked upper mandible, extraordinarily long wings and tail feathers.

one cup of coffee or tea to a meal. We used one cup of water every twenty-four hours to sponge our bodies over. This was always most refreshing. The pores of our skin would fairly eat the water up. Today on my watch I was looking at a nice dolphin fish[34] that was racing the boat, about six or eight feet down in the water, when suddenly I almost stopped breathing. Right below the canoe I saw the decks of a great big boat. I immediately brought the canoe up into the wind, and called Jack. For half an hour we crept up and down over that derelict, but could not find a clue as to its identity. It was apparently a cargo of lumber. Sometimes it would come to within fifteen feet of the surface, when again it would almost sink out of sight. It was quite uncanny, and would be a mean thing for some ship to hit.

August 23rd, I was lying in the bunk, when I saw Jack through the hatch sitting at the tiller with his knees across it holding it steady while he held his two hands in front of him. I could see nothing in his fingers and his hands were about six inches apart. He sat there utterly motionless, and with such a stare on his face that I quietly got up to the hatch and yet I could not see what he was looking at. I thought he must have hurt his hands, so stepping through the hatch, one step was enough to reach him, I took hold of his hands but could see nothing unusual. Then he held up to my eyes a long hair, quite apparently a woman's, also without doubt his wife's, the colour being distinctive. I went back into my bunk, no word to break Jack's dream did I utter. Forty-six days at sea and found—a lady's hair—a day to be remembered.

Under diary entry of the 23rd, we passed the equator and it also remarks about the Southern Cross. If your imagination is strong enough you can see the cross. The stars were not nearly as bright as they had been further north. It is astonishing how an ordinary layman

---

[34] A mammal resembling a porpoise but with a beak-like snout, edible, about seven feet long.

comes to know the stars. It is no trouble to steer by them, and much easier to look at them than a compass under a coal oil light.

For days past, three porpoises[35] had been drilling across the bow of our boat, two large ones and one just the size of a nice pig. I asked Jack if they were good to eat, and he said that he thought they were. So going forward to the foredeck where I often used to stretch out, I got the spear and shaft and tied the anchor rope to the thong of the spear. Several times the porpoises filed past right under the bow of the canoe, keeping rank like well-trained soldiers. I told myself just where I was going to stick baby porpoise, and then for one grand baby porpoise steak! Why I missed, I don't know, but underwater distance is very deceiving. Over its back I sent the spear, and hit papa an awful stab right behind where his shoulder should have been. How he went. The rope on the anchor flew, and it almost knocked me off the deck. Well, there is an end to everything, and the end of the slack in the rope came, and with it the *Tilikum* jibbed every one of her sails, with the darndest banging I ever heard. The jib roped around my head and I don't know yet why I didn't go overboard during the excitement, for by this time Mr. Porpoise was towing the canoe. Voss let an awful roar out of him, and over the cabin he came. He was furious. The boom of the mainsail had got him a good one right on the ear and his ear showed it. Often the boom used to wake me up when I would go to sleep, the canoe would come gently up into the wind, the boom being just the right height to hit you on the head.[36] Jack thought I had a whale I think, so instead of taking it easy and getting close to my game when I could easily have shot it, he cut with

---

[35] Small gregarious toothed whales, five to eight feet long, blackish above, white below.

[36] Voss in his book stated he threw a pail of water over Luxton when he fell asleep on watch, to which Luxton wrote: "No one threw any water. No one had to. If you dozed off, the boom of the mainsail soon woke you up when the *Tilikum* came up into the wind."

his knife and sacrificed both the anchor line, and worse still, my beloved harpoon. Well, that time I did tell him where to go! Later he apologized, as did I, and another breach was healed.

August 26th, we were strictly in the Southeast Trades, doing from one hundred and thirty to one hundred and seventy-five miles every day. We had passed Malden and Starbuck Islands. Nobody lived there and there was no anchorage. It would mean a swim for land, and as the sharks were large and hungry, and I was too thin for anything to eat, we passed these islands up, which are in the Line Islands and are British possessions.

August 27th, Jack figured that we were three days from Penrhyn Island. I hoped so, for we had not a gallon of water left. We caught a little rain last night but our rations, both water and food, were low. I thought if we got under a good rain storm and caught a few gallons of water, Jack would take a chance on the grub pile and try to make Samoa and pass up Penrhyn. He had been doing a lot of talking about man-eating savages and I knew there were none of that breed in this part of the ocean, and we certainly had not enough worldly goods to be killed for. I guess I told Jack pretty plain that one of the inducements of this voyage for me had been to see the islands. This was the first island we could possibly land at, and land at it I would. I pointed out to him that we were well armed, and the chances were that these natives would not be. Everything was in our favour to stand any number off in a running fight. But Jack had been reading the *South Pacific Ocean Directory*, and it was not encouraging to anyone, unless he was quite hungry, thirsty, and sick as I was. The directory read like this: "The last boat that passed this island, the ferocity of the savages precluded the possibility of attempting a landing." I tried to tell Jack that those words sounded far worse than they really were, but I could not comfort him one bit, until I suggested that we would make up a story that we were the forerunner of a British man-of-war and that the big guns would be along in a day or two. We would then try to get some water and food. If things did not look good we could beat it. This story apparently sounded fine to Jack, and he eventually consented to try a landing.

On the 29th of August the *Tilikum* reached the latitude that Penrhyn Island[37] is in. So, turning the canoe directly west, the island was supposed to be four degrees west of us. We sailed all that day and most of the next two days, wing and wing. She sure could scoot along, though she would rock like a baby's cradle. We eventually got used to it, and because we were making real time we did not mind the rolling. One thing about the *Tilikum* Voss had learned in his studious watches was that she could go faster with her bow lower in the water than her stern. Her bow was very sharp and came back in a knife-like blade shape, so that with what appeared to be a proper trim was only acting as a drag to her bottom.

Lowering the bow cut a wider swath of water for her stern to follow in. Jack discovered this one day when I was cleaning out the aft hold, and I moved most of the ship's supplies from there to the fore of the cabin. After that Voss always sailed her very low in the bow.

On the morning of September 2nd, I had just finished washing the breakfast dishes and was wondering if the watch-chronometer would be honest in its time, when suddenly Jack yelled out "Land ahead!"

"Yes," I said, "so is the South Pole."

---

[37] Penrhyn, one of the Cook Islands or Hervey Archipelago.

VII

Tamarii Tahiti

Penrhyn island. Something real to see. We enter the lagoon.
Pigs, chickens, cats, but no people. We get a scare.
The wonder-vessel we find in the lagoon, and something of
her people. The old time trader, and early conditions on
Penrhyn. Something of Bully Hayes.

T he watch we used for a chronometer I took out of a gold case
that I had been wearing for several years. I had William L.
Challoner[38] in Victoria set it in a screw back and front in the
case, and all the time we were building the canoe on Queen
Charlotte Sound he was regulating it. I must say he made a good job

---

[38] See *Victoria Daily Times* (Victoria, B.C.) July 6, 1914, p. 14 (obituary). William

L. Challoner, of Challoner and Mitchell, Jewellers. Challoner was born in Strathroy,

Ontario, 1865. Trained in jewellery business in London, Ontario. He and Mitchell

founded the firm in Strathroy. After five years moved to Victoria, and ended twenty-

seven years of partnership when they retired in 1912. Challoner died July 5, 1914.

of it. Not once during our whole voyage did it ever lead the canoe astray. Penrhyn was the only port we ever ran down on latitude. Still thinking Jack was kidding me about the land, I did not hurry with my work. I finally came on deck and sure enough, about six miles off I could see palm trees growing right out of the water. Gradually the trees kept getting higher, until we could see the waves breaking on the reefs. Not for over an hour did I take my eyes off those trees. Nothing in my whole life ever looked quite so good. Jack could have lost a dozen spears right then and it would never have bothered me. He started to say something about the *South Sea Directory* and savages, and all I did was look at him and he shut up. That was the last I ever heard of not landing on Penrhyn.

For a mile or two, two or three times, we sailed up and down the ocean side of the island. We could see nothing of people although houses were plainly visible through the beautiful groves of coconut palms. At last we decided to sail through the entrance of the lagoon, this entrance being on the northwest side. Voss was at the tiller and I stood on the foredeck to watch for shoal water. Several times the bottom of the entrance seemed very close, but it was more of a rush through heavy ground swell, and we soon shot into the deeper waters of the lagoon. What a picture was before us. Along a wonderful beach were dozens and dozens of canoes, and anchored out close to the shore were a dozen or two white, board built sailing boats, from eighteen to twenty feet long with one mast and a wide beam. These man-eaters sure had good taste about sailing boats. In among the palm trees, which were a hundred feet or more in height, were all kinds of houses, well built and stuccoed with coral, or walled with the leaves of the palms. All kinds of colours and sizes of chickens could be seen and quite a number of pigs, what breed no one could guess. There was no sign of any human being. All this time the *Tilikum* was sailing up and down in front of the village, inviting attention from someone, anyone. What a liar that *Pacific Directory* must be.

Set back a little further among the palms than some of the houses was a building that stood out very conspicuously on account of its size. It had a very high pitched roof, quite fifty by eighty or ninety feet and rough cast sides made of coral and lime. Suddenly, out of this church-like construction swarmed the humans that the rest of the setting lacked. They swarmed in such numbers that I quite made up my mind that Samoa was good enough for me, water or no water. They were all running, rushing towards us and the beach and in no time every canoe was manned and afloat, everyone paddling frantically toward the prize and a dinner, and that prize and dinner was nothing other than the *Tilikum* and her crew. I asked Voss if he knew an entrance other than the one we had come in by, and he said perhaps he did so invited me to the forward deck to watch the shoal water. The canoe had a fair wind and no man-eater could go as fast as we did. Perhaps half to three-quarters of a mile we had sailed when uncovering part of the lagoon that had been hitherto hidden by the point of an island, there at anchor was the most beautiful two-masted schooner it was ever my pleasure to see. At her main mast flew the flag of the Republic of France. I yelled to Voss but he had already seen her. He sailed a little further, holding his course on the same wind, when he yelled to me, "Jab all sail." It was the only time I ever knew him to do it, and away we were to a fair and fast course to the schooner.

All I could see on her deck were natives, and two in particular stood out conspicuously. One was a very tall man with heavy angular features and a dark complexion. Even at a distance I noticed his skin. The other was a man of about five foot eleven inches, not looking so tall on account of his girth, and both were dressed in white drill pants and shirts. The rest of the crowd were naked, except for loin cloths which were of many colours. What a picture they made. It was the whitest boat I had ever seen, and in such a wonderful setting with palm trees behind it. In the lee of the island she gently bowed to the swell of the Pacific. Not a soul moved on board the schooner, yet it was all there, water and food, and companionship that no human can live without.

"Ship ahoy," in mighty good English, the best I had heard since the wife of the captain of the *Mary Winkelman* had kidded me about leaving home. "Do you want a line? Do you want to come on board?" came across that trade wind-swept lagoon. In a second we were under her stern. A line was thrown from the schooner's deck, which I quickly tied around the mainmast. We were up on deck by the rope ladder hanging from the bulwark, and, before you could count to five, over the schooner's side. My! What a ship, the most particular could eat off the boards of her deck. Clean was no name for it, the heart of the tree those boards came from was never more white.

I heard "Will you come below?" and on looking up, before me was the stoutest of the pants wearers, speaking to me. He was quite as dark as the lightest of these islanders, and spoke in perfect English, but apparently a native, so all combined, caused me to pause before accepting. Leading the way down a broad companion staircase into one of the most commodious and comfortable staterooms, this English-speaking native asked me to be seated. At the far end of the room, which reached to both sides of the vessel and about eighteen feet long, was a huge white bed with coverings that quite matched all the rest of the furnishings of this wonder cabin. At the far end and past the berth was the most disreputable looking character I had seen in many a long day, quite out of keeping with any of the rest of the company. He had long hair, a frizzly ill-kempt beard, a dirty shirt and worse overalls of no particular colour, and he was barefooted as well. While I stood staring at this individual and my "native" host was talking to one of the crew in a language I could not understand, there suddenly appeared Voss, coming towards me, from the same end of the stateroom where the tramp was standing. Not until I heard his voice behind me was I aware of the mirror. I was looking at my own reflection. I was the dirty, ill-kept tramp. The *Tilikum* carried no mirrors. I think Voss was afraid one might get broken, so not for at least fifty-eight days had I seen myself. The last time was at dear old McKenzie's trading store, at Village Island. Voss was a little king alongside of me, because I had a short time previous to making Penrhyn, insisted on trimming his beard and hair, telling him that such a job was easy for a naturalist.

"Well, gentlemen, I see your boat is the *Tilikum*, where in Hell did you come from?" boomed forth that delightful English accent. I was quite content to sit there and listen and almost forgot my thirst I was so glad to hear someone talk, until down the companionway came a native with coconuts, and a quart bottle of claret on a tray. He handed each of us one coconut with the end neatly cut off. They were as soft as a shell-skinned, hard-boiled egg. I watched my host; he drank two or three big swallows from the coconut and reaching for the claret bottle, he filled the nut to the brim. I was not slow in following his actions. Never, never in my life before or since was there such a drink and never will it be forgotten. The cure was worth the torture of thirst and hunger. I consumed easily a dozen coconuts in that hour's talk with Captain Winchester,[39] Englishman sure he was, a thoroughbred at that, tanned as dark as any native, but at that not so dark as I. "Children of Tahiti," *Tamarii Tahiti*, his beautiful ship was called. It was perhaps nine hundred tons, a dream of a ship. She was registered out of Papeete, Tahiti, Society Islands, of French possession.

---

[39] Letter from Captain James N. Hall to Norman Luxton, Papeete, January 9, 1926. "Mrs. Winchester has asked me to reply to your recent letter to the Captain. . . . I know how sorry you will be to learn that good old Captain Joe is dead. He died in April 1923, during a voyage he made from Tahiti to Samoa, and is buried at Apia. . . . During the last four years of his life he was skipper of the *Tahitian Maiden*, a three masted schooner, belonging to the Pacific Coconut Products Company."

He could hardly believe we had come from Vancouver Island, and when I told him of the bluff story we intended to put up to the natives to secure water and provisions he laughed heartily. Then he suddenly sobered and said, "When I call the boy down again, tell me that story and tell it as if it were true. Tell it, by God, as if you meant every word of it." I did not know what he meant, but knowing he was in earnest, I described a man-of-war that I had seen in Esquimalt. All this time he held the boy for our orders of coconuts. I think that I ordered six, my capacity was unlimited. The boy disappeared to reappear with our orders. After him, down the companionway came the tall dark man, who wore the only other pair of pants I had seen on board. Captain Winchester introduced him to us as Captain Tepau,[40] called Pau, and he was no ordinary native. He was heir apparent to the Tahitian throne, being cousin to the present king of Tahiti who, poor devil, was in one of the French penal islands. Pau was quite excited with the news that a British man-of-war would be along soon. I caught something about someone "being released," that Penrhyn would receive some justice it had never expected, and something about "its chief getting some of his own medicine." I must have by this time looked quite puzzled. Pau was not talking in English, so Captain Winchester was good enough to explain just what Pau was speaking about. Captain Winchester's partner, Captain Dexter,[41] had

---

[40] Letter from Captain Winchester to Norman Luxton, Papeete, October 12, 1921. "Poor old Pau has gone to join his boss and friend."

[41] *Ibid.* "That Prince among Men, my friend and partner, George Dexter, lost his life on the schooner *Tahiti Girl* in a hurricane in the Poumotus on the 13th of January 1906. I am sure that a man like him knew no fear of having a good place in the next world. God rest his soul. . . . After you left Penrhyn we amalgamated our business with S. R. Maxwell and Company Ltd. I being a large shareholder was in command of *Tamarii Tahiti* and anchored off the island of Tackume when the wind shifted and drove me on shore a total loss. . . . Since then I have been Sailing Master out of the Port of Papeete."

THE DEPARTURE

Tilikum at Oak Bay, Victoria, on May 20, 1901. In the foreground are Mrs. Voss and family. The men from left to right are: O. B. Ormond, N. K. Luxton and J. C. Voss.

Photograph: Provincial Archives, Victoria, B.C.

NORMAN KENNY LUXTON
Looking gaunt and still recuperating from the reef disaster that
forced him to terminate his adventure at Suva, Fiji, on October
18, 1901.

Photograph: Adelaide Photo Co., Sydney, Australia

NORMAN KENNY LUXTON
Enjoying Banff Indian Days circa 1950.
Photograph: Calgary Herald

APIA HARBOUR
Civilization at Samoa in 1901.
Photograph: Norman Luxton

NATIVE VILLAGE
Situated near Apia.

Photograph: Norman Luxton

Tᴵʟɪᴋᴜᴍ ᴀᴛ Sᴀᴍᴏᴀ
Still appearing "shipshape" after such a voyage.
Photograph: Provincial Archives, Victoria, B.C.

TILIKUM AT CAPETOWN

Displayed on the beach at Table Bay in 1903. The ravages of time, the sea and the reef near Suva, Fiji, are showing on the bow section.

Photograph: Provincial Archives, Victoria, B.C.

NATIVE BOAT
Seen by Luxton at Samoa.
Photograph: Norman Luxton

ROBERT LOUIS STEVENSON
The trail to his grave. Stevenson and family lived from 1890 until
his death in 1894 at Vailima, his house in Samoa.

Photograph: Norman Luxton

UNKNOWN ARTIST'S SKETCH
Showing *Tilikum* under sail.
Photograph: Provincial Archives, Victoria, B.C.

TILIKUM ON EXHIBIT
At Table Bay, Capetown, in 1903, long after Luxton's departure.
Photograph: Provincial Archives, Victoria, B.C.

A POST CARD
Tilikum at Margate Harbour, England, in 1905.

Photograph: Provincial Archives, Victoria, B.C.

that morning been seized, for the divers of the *Tamarii* had refused to cease fishing pearl shell in the lagoon in spite of orders from the island chief. At the time of our entrance into the lagoon every man, woman, and child was at Dexter's trial in the huge house that was so conspicuous. He had been condemned to be thrown into the northwest passage that night, with a big stone tied to his neck. Our story of the man-of-war had been blown to the island faster than believable, for over the deck we heard Dexter coming down the stairway booming all the time. He was the biggest, best natured looking man that I ever met. My, how he was roasting the kinglets of every island in the Pacific, backwards, forwards and sideways, laughing all the time, and blaming his release to his own bluffing. Not until his partner had told him of the man-of-war, did he stop laughing, then only for a minute, when I am quite sure all the fish in the lagoon must have left in fear and trembling. Never was there such laughter. He rolled, he rocked, he cried and made us all do likewise, but it was a great excuse to order a dozen more coconuts. Now here is the strange part of my story. Forty-eight hours afterwards a British gunboat appeared away across the lagoon, at the entrance to the southwest passage. There had not been one there for eighteen years, but this is all in the story and must come in its proper term. How glad, and surprised, I was that I was not a liar.

Let me now tell you something about the old time traders, both as to their business and character.

Captain Winchester was a native of Liverpool. Following the life of the sea, he first found Papeete some twenty years before I met him. There he stayed, seeing the wonderful chance of a trading business to be developed throughout the islands in copra and pearl shell. His dream came true, for with hard work and by treating the islanders with all fairness, he and his partner Captain Dexter were loved and respected wherever their trading boat let down its anchor. From a small one sail eighty ton schooner, in twenty years these men boasted the finest nine hundred ton, two mast schooner in the South Seas, and well stocked trading stores in many islands, wherever the population demanded them.

Captain Dexter was a half-cast Tahitian and a graduate from some California university. For forty-five to fifty years these men held the respect of all who knew them, and died loved and honoured by the natives among whom their lives had been spent.

I had the great pleasure of meeting Mrs. Winchester[42] at Penrhyn, and a more delightful lady I never knew. What a wonderful woman. I could well understand Winchester, English gentleman and sailor, willing and even glad to sever all his home connections to marry this native lady of Tahiti. A faithful and good wife she proved to be and during the war of 1914 to 1918, she loaned the allies no less than four of her sons, two boys in France, one in the New Zealand army and one in the African army. The youngest was just over fifteen years old, and all of them got recognitions for bravery. It is no wonder that years after in 1922, J. Winchester writing to me said, "Even though I have had bad luck with my ships, I am away ahead of the game by having a wonderful wife."

Dexter and Winchester really belonged to the newer era of traders. These men enlisted pretty much from all civilized countries and all classes. Honesty is always the leading requisite in dealing with any natives, and all these men possessed it, or otherwise they would pass so quickly, their names would have soon been forgotten. Many exhibited educated tastes, and in this category Winchester and Dexter loomed large. It was with considerable pleasure I presented to Winchester my set of Rudyard Kipling, the only books I had on board besides the Bible.

---

[42] See letter from Mrs. James N. Hall (daughter of Mrs. Winchester), Papeete, March 28, 1969. Mrs. Winchester died in Papeete, Tahiti, on November 1, 1951.

I was guest and comrade to many of these traders for months. I saw them at their best and at their worst. The latter usually happened on the arrival of visitors at their island. The drinking was always a mild affair, yes, very mild indeed, compared with any parties held in our cities of America. Swearing was indulged in heartily. But it was a poor judge of human nature who could not appreciate the manly qualities which the rough exterior covered but could not conceal. I had read a great deal of these so-called whisky traders, and had even heard them denounced at illustrated lantern slides lectures, but such denunciations are impossible to believe when once you have met these men in person. Such a man was George Ellis of Manihiki Island. According to his own diary, it seems that George was a mere lad in 1865 when he shipped as a cabin boy to the East Pacific. The vessel he was on was seeking native labour for Peru. Ellis, not liking the company nor the ship's business, deserted at the first possible chance, which was Caroline Island, about four hundred miles east of Penrhyn. Building himself a ten-ton cutter, with the help of some other castaways on Caroline Island, they sailed to Penrhyn. There they found the island people in great sorrow. The natives had been working on Tahiti and on returning had found their island depopulated of all but children and the old by Peruvian kidnappers, who had taken them to Callao for plantation work, never to return to their native islands. If by force these men and women could not be put on board, the slavers made wonderful promises of gifts and eating, and when once decoyed to the ship, it was a simple matter to make them prisoners. Thus, Ellis says, Penrhyn was almost depopulated at the time of his arrival, at least two thousand having been stolen away. Penrhyn was not the only island to suffer, and in a short time the slavers had to go afield, much farther west, as the smaller islands soon had no more desirable labour. "However," Ellis goes on, "friends were not the only ones stolen. Enemies alike filled the want of Peruvian planters, so that in one way it proved a blessing."

The Penrhyn natives were forever fighting. It seems that there were eight or nine different tribes who spent all their spare time fighting and quarrelling amongst themselves. The rows, says Ellis's diary, were always about land or women, fishing and pearl shell rights. The quarrels would grow very bitter sometimes, and raiding parties would steal out at night and cut their neighbours' coconut trees down. This would be followed by a real battle to the death, many being killed, but never the women and children. They were always spared, eventually to become part of the conquering tribe.

Ellis was the first white man to make his home on Penrhyn Island, and although he was an old man at the time I saw him, it was not hard to see what he had been thirty years before. He must have possessed lots of pluck, and fair dealing, so characteristic of all the successful pioneers who dealt equal justice to all. With such a code a white man could go far in the South Seas. It was not long before Ellis was made a chief. He taught them all he knew, especially that of boat-building and sail-making. Ellis was a godsend to these natives, as this was before missionaries had established churches or schools. So this rough and ready sailor gave the Penrhyn and Manihiki natives their first grounding in so-called civilization, and who will deny it was not even a better one than verse and prayer.

How different to Ellis were such characters as Bully Hayes.[43] It was fortunate that such rowdies as Hayes were few and far between and more so that their lives while merry and wild were generally of short duration.

---

[43] James A. Michener and A. Grove Day, *Rascals in Paradise* (London: Secker and Warburg, 1957), Chap. VII, "Bully Hayes: South Sea Buccaneer," pp. 223–58. William Henry Hayes, or "Bully" Hayes as he was more popularly known, was born in Cleveland, Ohio, in 1829 and was murdered at sea in 1877. See also *ibid.*, pp. 370–71.

George Ellis[44] told me that he killed Bully Hayes, but of this assertion I could only get native corroboration. Ellis insisted that one day while sailing with Hayes out of Samoa and even before Ellis settled in Penrhyn, Hayes had enticed a daughter of one of George's native friends on board, this unknown to George until they had been at sea some time. Ellis remonstrated with Hayes, asking him to return to Apia and give the girl back to her parents. He said Hayes was really crazy at times. Losing his head completely, on Ellis's demands, he rushed down the companionway and was coming back with a pistol to shoot Ellis, when Ellis grabbed a marlinspike and bashed Hayes's head in. Ellis returned to Samoa and was greatly honoured by the natives for ridding the ocean of a nuisance and terror to everyone.

Such was the story that George Ellis gave me of Hayes. From one end of the Pacific to the other, Bully Hayes's name may still be heard. It must have been some fifty years after his time that I had landed in his old stamping ground. I found it almost impossible to get true and authentic stories about him, and therefore I cannot resist copying from one of George Ellis's books a short account of the kind of man Hayes was. This book was written, I think, by F. J. Moss[45] of New Zealand. I trust he will forgive the liberty taken. The book was old and almost unreadable, so I am only guessing that he was the author.

---

[44] See letter from Captain Winchester to Norman Luxton, Papeete, October 2, 1921. Luxton's high opinion of Ellis was evidently not shared by Winchester: "By a curious coincidence a boat arrived from Manihiki the day after I got your letter with the man you met here [George Ellis], of course he is an old liar, but he was on board Bully Hayes' schooner as a boy when they killed Hayes, and has come to consider it was he who did it."

[45] Frederick J. Moss, *Through Atolls and Islands in the Great South Sea* (London: Sampson Low, 1889), pp. 84–92. Bully Hayes is mentioned in Chap. IV, "Some Old-fashioned Celebrities."

He writes:

Hayes was quite a big, bald-headed man, weighing perhaps two hundred pounds with soft eyes and persuading ways. He was an American. Called "the magnetic type and mad as a hatter at times," said one of the men who sailed with him. Hayes made his first colonial appearance in 1864 at Invercargill, in South New Zealand, with a small travelling musical company. Afterwards he was captain of a collier[46] and he traded between Australia and New Zealand. After the Maori War he was strongly suspected of providing the natives with powder and lead, landed at out of the way places on the coast. His practice, it is now known, was to spread the powder under the cabin and carelessly litter the floor with straw. No official visitor would dream that powder would be hidden in so dangerous a place. The Maori War ended, Hayes started for Tahiti to begin on new lines. But his ship foundered at sea near the lagoon island of Manihiki, where he was most kindly treated by the people, who helped him to build another small craft. The little vessel finished, Hayes started out with her and a party of Manihiki natives, for a marriage feast, on Rakahanga Island,[47] and ultimately found himself at Samoa. There he enticed the hapless natives to engage for work on one of the plantations, not forgetting to charge their employers a good round sum for the expenses he was put to in bringing the reapers to Samoa. ("What an infernal scoundrel!" I could not help injecting as he went on.) Hayes had once left a man on the little island of Ujelang to get copra for him.

"There were only a few there," said the party, "but he never came near me again. I was nearly dead, living on fish and coconuts and tormented with anxiety to get away. At last by great good luck, a vessel called and rescued me. I never saw Hayes afterwards, but if he were to come here only to slap me on the back, with one of his jovial laughs and start talking and

---

[46] Coal ship.

[47] Rakahanga Island, South Pacific, between Penrhyn and Manihiki.

chaffing me about Ujelang, I wouldn't say to you that you mightn't see me shaking hands with him in less than ten minutes, and attempt to talk to him about being left on Ujelang."[48]

"Well," I [Moss] replied, "there is no accounting for these things in your case but I should certainly have a very different settlement with him."

"Ah!" said my friend, "you do not know Hayes, or you would not talk that way."

I was happy to say that I did not know him, and that unless a Governor of one of H.M. gaols, I should not care for the honour. My friend shook his head and said that all this was not proof against Hayes, like that captain of H.M.S. *Rosario*[49] who was supposed to cover the Pacific hunting for Hayes. At one time, Hayes happened to be at the island of Kusaie,[50] when the *Rosario* called, he had just lost his little vessel *Leonore* close to that island and had heard about the *Rosario*. He went boldly on board and asked about charges which he was told had been made against him and also offered his services to pilot her into harbour, if they thought a pilot necessary. Then Hayes contrived to get one of his leading accusers made drunk on board. The drunken man disgusted the captain of the *Rosario*, who was finally so taken by Hayes ingenious manner and abstemiousness (for he never drank), that he allowed him to go ashore to bring back papers necessary for his defence. Hayes left in a small boat owned by a native friend. The friend returned with the sad story that the boat had been smashed on landing and he himself was badly bruised, as he showed, but poor Hayes, he feared, must have been stunned for he sank and had not reappeared. Nor did he reappear, until ten days after the *Rosario's* departure. Then he took passage in a whaling ship to Guam, in the

---

[48] One of the Marshall Islands, North Pacific.

[49] See Michener and Day, *op. cit.* Captain A. E. Dupuis of the *Rosario*. H.M.S. *Rosario* was a sloop built at Deptford, England, in 1860, 673 tons, 154 h.p., which, in the 1870's, was in Australian or South Pacific waters. It was sold out of service in 1882.

[50] One of the Caroline Islands, North Pacific.

Ladrones,[51] where he got in trouble with Spanish authorities and was sent to prison at Manila. He there became a rigid and pious Congregationalist in great favour with an American mission. After, at Manila, he became a Catholic and through the representation of Spanish priests, was soon released and sent on his way to San Francisco. At San Francisco, Hayes contrived by trickery to get possession of a cutter yacht, which he called the *Lotus*. The fellow evidently had poetry in him, with his *Lotus* and *Leonore*. He provided her with stores by taking them, without leave, from a California Lighthouse, and began a new career of adventure and rascality. The crew consisted only of himself and a native and a Scandinavian named Peter, who is now living on one of the Caroline Islands. They got to Jaluit,[52] and at once had trouble leaving the island. Peter was at the helm when Hayes in a violent rage went below for a pistol to shoot him. Arming himself with the iron boom crutch, Peter struck him down as, pistol in hand, Hayes put his head above the companion. Thus without more ado, he threw Hayes and pistol overboard. He took the *Lotus* back to Jaluit, and reported what had occurred.

Of Hayes feats of roguery, I heard everywhere, how he partly bought and partly stole from the French owner, the vessel which he called the *Cruiser*. How he stole a cutter in the Gulf of Siam and voluntarily gave her as atonement to a man whom he had wronged, accompanying the gift with astounding accounts of cost and quality; how he got in trouble at Samoa, by using for illegal purposes the *Atlantic* of which he was master; how he was made prisoner by the council to be dealt with by the man-of-war, and how instead of waiting for the man-of-war, he took a sudden passage for Shanghai on the *Pioneer*, with Captain Pease, a man as lawless and unscrupulous as himself. The account of Hayes career would be incomplete without giving subsequent dealing in the *Pioneer*, for with this vessel he started on an entirely new course. The owners of the *Pioneer* were merchants in Shanghai. They had

---

[51] Ladrones Islands, now known as the Mariana Islands, North Pacific.

[52] Jaluit Atoll in the Marshall Islands.

failed and the estate was in the hands of trustees. This old vessel was going to waste and she was in every way as dilapidated as possible. The crew (Manila men and other natives), were told by Hayes to protest against the vessel being sold or given back to assignees in Shanghai; and so threatened with lawsuits and probable cost of repairing the vessel, they let him have her for a nominal sum. Of this a very small portion was paid in cash, and the rest it is needless to say, was never paid at all.

To re-engage a crew and repair the ship was an affair of little time. She was renamed the *Leonore*. Conversant with all the affairs of the involved firm, Hayes went by their trading stations on the islands, protested formally, wound up their business; and obtained from the changes what supply of goods they had on hand, and what balance in cash they were able to pay. Among his victims on this occasion was Alfred Restiaux. From him and many others, I had the account now put all together, and which, I believe, presents accurately the strange content of unblushing roguery, rough minds and strong sentiments dashed with insanity, which formed a character, whose notoriety the like has not been seen before, nor happily can ever be seen again on the Pacific.

VIII

Island Diversions

*Early life of Dexter and Winchester at Penrhyn.
Dexter to be killed, arrival of H.M.S. Torch. A wonderful
boat and a new man. Pearl shell fishing and the divers.
On the bottom of the lagoon. I see the Hula-Hula.
Something about babies. A princess is offered to me in
marriage or otherwise. I accept conditionally.*

The origin offered of the Pacific Island races is as many as there are islands in the sea; of their starting point no ethnologists will agree. One thing we do know is that they have supplied a great deal to the commerce of the world in the shape of coconuts, pearl shell, which has many by-products, sandalwood, which is all but gone, and poetry and stories by the ream. In latter years there have been sugar cane, cocoa, cotton, tobacco and many other things cultivated with some success. Of all the Atoll Islands where *Tilikum* called, possibly Penrhyn and Manihiki were the most interesting, so of these two islands I will chiefly make my story.

It seems that some twenty-five years before the *Tilikum* arrived at Penrhyn, Dexter and Winchester were trading in a small way through the islands lying closest to Tahiti, when about 1878 a small barque blew into Penrhyn, and though not a complete wreck much might have been saved had not the natives beached her and completed what the waves and weather had not finished. For several years the captain of the barque lived quietly on Penrhyn Island and finally, on the arrival of a British man-of-war, he laid his story before the commander of the war boat. A trial was held, the island was found guilty, and complete recompense was ordered by the British commander. The island at that time was not so rich in copra, pearl, or money as in later times, and they were utterly unable to pay. Dexter and Winchester being on the spot soon made arrangements with the island chief to pay the fines of the court, but in return they must have the privilege of a trading post and certain pearl fishing rights in the lagoon for a term of twenty years. For years this agreement was kept, and the island people were much improved by Dexter's and Winchester's store and advice. Coconut groves were cultivated as never before, and the lagoon was never stripped of all its shells.

Natives of the South Seas are really like children, and sometimes badly raised children. Forgetting the lean days of twenty years before and the wealth that Dexter and Winchester had brought to the island, they ordered the store seized and at the first opportunity they also seized Dexter because he refused to stop fishing pearl in the lagoon, having still two years to complete the contract. He was then condemned to death by the islanders in the novel and no doubt painless manner of having a large-sized coral stone tied to his neck, and then thrown into the passage-way that joined the ocean and the lagoon. By putting Captain Dexter in the passage-way he would cease very quickly to be a possible nuisance, but if otherwise thrown into the lagoon he might bob up in the morning when the ladies of the village were observing their ablutions on the beach before breakfast, and might thus spoil their appetite. In the passage-way the current was strong, sharks were many and hungry, and the devil fish had a cluster of caves all their own. The natives had apparently become quite fearless of any retribution that might fall on their heads. For eighteen years no British boat had called, surely "Preitane" (Britain) had forgotten their very existence, so they would kick this silly contract overboard and take all the pearl shell themselves. Such, indeed, was the very unpleasant proposed disposal of Captain Dexter, when suddenly out of the blue appeared a forerunner of a British man-of-war, in the shape of the *Tilikum*. The "boat was upset" and the chief and his councillors found themselves in rough water. Dexter was released at once, and forty-eight hours later my cock-and-bull story came true, and Her Majesty's gunboat *Torch*[53] was only waiting for a pilot to cast her anchor in the lagoon.

There was certainly consternation in the village, for no one knew quite what would happen. A South Sea island is a hard place to

---

[53] M. N. Watt, comp. *Index to the N-Z Section of the Register of All British Ships, 1840–1950* (Wellington, New Zealand: New Zealand Ship and Marine Society, 3963), Part I, p. 543. "*Rama*: Official Number 121394, steamer, 610.09 gross tonnage; 244.25 registered tonnage. 181 x 14.5 ft. 1 engine, 93 h.p. Built at Sheerness by the Admiralty. Originally the H.M.S. *Torch*. Registered No. 2/1920(7/xii/20) Port of Wellington (Initial Registry). Ship totally lost at the Chatham Islands on 18/xi/1924." See also, Charles W. N. Ingram and Percival O. Wheatley, *New Zealand Shipwrecks, 1795–1960*, 3rd ed. (Wellington, New Zealand: Reed, 1961), p. 346. "The *Rama*, No. 121394, was a screw steamer of 610 tons gross and 244 tons net register, built at His Majesty's Dockyards, Sheerness, in 1895, and her dimensions were: length 181.5, beam 32 ft., depth 14.5 ft., her engines were of 93 h.p. As Her Majesty's gunboat *Torch*, the *Rama* served for a considerable period as a warship on the New Zealand coast. When it was judged that her usefulness as a warship was at an end she was dismantled and fitted with refrigerating machinery for the carrying of fish, and ran for some time under the aegis of the Chatham Islands Fishing Company."

hide. It is only a few feet above sea level, with no grass, nothing in fact to hide behind but coconut trees. Indeed, the tops would prove a much better place, but then it blows continually, and land crab holes were out of the question to crawl into, so the chief and his councillors decided not to run. Commander MacAllister invited them to attend court in the very house where they had condemned Captain Dexter. The case lasted eight days as eighteen years had to be rehashed, tons of shell reweighed, lagoon rights visited, but the answer in the end was very plain. Damages and bodily harm to the tune of seventy-six thousand Mexican dollars was what Dexter and Winchester received. This was all paid in Mexican silver, cartwheels and halves, all packed in little sacks and carried to the beach, one sack each on a man's shoulder, and delivered on board the *Children of Tahiti*. So rich and prosperous had the island government become, that this seventy-six thousand Mexican dollars, taken from the treasury, hardly made a dent in the pile.

After drinking more coconuts and claret than I ever thought I could hold, Captain Winchester took Jack and me over to his trading store at the village and presented us to his head store-keeper, Mr. Macdonald, and told him to both clothe us and make us all over again. At the time I did not realize the great favour conferred upon us, as fresh water is about the scarcest thing there is on a lagoon island. Yet Winchester ordered his manager to bathe us. Only in rainy season was such a luxury as a bath enjoyed. Out behind the store was a big iron tank used to store rain-water and this water was as precious as the very pearls in the lagoon. Economy was practised and water was doled out only as a drinking fluid. But not today, orders were orders, so into a couple of large wooden tubs we climbed. They were over half-filled and when we were in only our chins were above water. No snakes had anything on us, we shed more hide than any tannery ever had in its vats. I positively went to sleep in mine and perhaps the coconuts I had consumed helped me to my slumbers.

When I awoke, Jack was gone and Macdonald was standing by the tub laughing his head off. A pair of scissors, razor, brush and soap were on a stool, as well as a tooth brush, clean towels, drill pants, a silk shirt and a pair of canvas shoes. They certainly looked inviting, but for another hour I refused to move. Scrubbing and ducking, I could never get enough of that water and soap. Finally I climbed out, dressed in the pants and shoes and, with towels over my shoulders, I got Macdonald to shave me and cut my hair. He was a real artist at the game. I then put on my shirt and when I walked out I was as light as air, at least so I felt, and this time it was no coconut inspiration. The first man I met in front of the store was Winchester. He looked me over for a minute and said, "Did you come in on the *Tilikum*?"

"Have you forgotten my name?" I asked.

Then he laughed, "Really, you know, I did not know you."

The next ten days I saw the captains only at meal times on the *Children of Tahiti*, their court case taking up most of their time. Here on this wonder-boat, I slept and ate, spending the evenings on Mrs. Winchester's verandah, listening to the singing of the natives who used to cluster in front of the house and sing and dance the night away. What happy mortals they were, with not a care in the world.

During the day I spent most of my time in one of the white pearling boats on the lagoon, watching the natives dive for pearl shell. With a glass-bottom box the diver would jump into the lagoon, looking down through this box sunk partly in the water. With his head where the cover of the box might have been, he could easily spot a pearl shell on the bottom of the lagoon. Then down he would go many feet, quite as gracefully as any fish, and stay so long that I often thought he must be drowned. But always back to the surface he would come and out of a bag he carried at his waist he would put into the boat half a dozen or more huge pearl oysters, all cut away with a knife from their resting places among the coral. Naked divers of Penrhyn Island are known the South Seas over for their great ability at this art of pearl fishing. The same success applies to their boat-building and sailing. No island in the South Seas has their equal. Depth of water in diving has no terror for them, though the average time a man can spend at this game is four years. To overcome this one obstacle of so short a time for valuable divers, Dexter and Winchester invented a simple and useful diving outfit. The ordinary diver's costume was so heavy and cumbersome—that was forty years ago—a man so dressed could not move into the many shapes neces-sary to collect pearl oysters. The bottom of Penrhyn Island lagoon was anything but smooth. In other words, it was no sandy beach but on the contrary full of coral crevices, holes, pillars and obstacles such as only coral can build, so that really it took a naked man all his time to move around and get these hidden shells.

Taking the lightest possible head-piece of a diver's outfit, fitting the usual air hose etc. to it, Dexter and Winchester then fastened to the neck of the head-piece a waterproof shirt-shaped garment made of canvas. There was also a pair of overalls that did not necessarily have to be worn and the usual weighted boots, then the diver was ready to work. A belt around the waist drew the shirt in tightly to the body, so that no air would escape. The wrists of the shirt were free; in such a manner so loose and easy was the suit made that the diver had the full use of all his limbs and could crawl around underneath the water almost as well as the naked divers.

It was in such an outfit that Captain Dexter's brother[54] introduced me to the bottom of the lagoon, and I was assured that if any shark came near me all I had to do was raise my arm and he would swim to any place I might point. This Dexter was just as funny as his captain

---

[54] Letter from Captain Winchester to Norman Luxton, Papeete, October 12, 1921. "Jimmy Dexter is still alive and doing fairly well." See also, Letter from Mrs. James N. Hall, Papeete, April 28, 1969. "James Dexter died on the 30th of April, 1942, and is buried in Papeete Cemetery."

brother, but his practical jokes were more serious sometimes than funny. However, I was game to try it once. So, carefully listening to instructions about life-line, hose, signals etc., a prayer was said and the glass was screwed on the helmet in front of my face. Then, taking a high step off the deck of the boat, and bringing my feet together as quickly as possible I sank, feet first, through the lagoon waters, with the most awful roaring in my head that I ever experienced. I hit the bottom right side up, at a depth of about twenty feet or so, in one of the most beautiful soft lights I have ever experienced. I felt strange, but quite all right. Dexter had picked the spot in the lagoon for my descent and had pretty much told me which way to go. Standing still a minute to get my bearing, I was suddenly conscious of fish of every size and shape all around me, but nothing so large that you could not eat it. Some did not look like fish at all, but more like something alive and moving. I had landed on an apparently barren bottom, so moving along in the direction Dexter had told me to go I came to the original "Alice's Wonderland." Here all the South Sea colours were again, worked out this time in coral, actually in truly miniature forests, just like a second growth of our Rocky Mountain pines and spruces. There were little trees and big trees, crooked trees and some perfect Christmas tree shapes, all in white and coloured corals; and in among it all these countless coloured fish, all taking me in, as if I were some kind of a freak. Well, I hope they enjoyed my company as much as I did theirs, although I certainly quite unintentionally scared them properly. Raising my arm to adjust the head-piece, my open sleeve released a bubble of air from the shirt sleeve. How they scooted, I'm sure more than one barked its shins on the coral. Several times I went down to the floor of the lagoon, even gathering some pearl oysters once. I never met a shark but there were plenty of small fish. Standing perfectly still, they would nose the glass of the helmet. They must have all been lady fish they were so very inquisitive. I could never get over feeling that there was always something behind me, and cased up in that helmet you could only see ahead. Big sharks and devil fish were always at my back, that was the only unpleasant feeling I had when walking the lagoon.

When the pearl oysters were collected they were piled on a sunny beach, where they soon opened and died. It was never hard to tell where the oyster beach was. It reeked to heaven with its smells. Yet, every bit of the meat had to be fingered and thumbed to find, if possible, another pearl. Pearls were not so plentiful even thirty years ago at Penrhyn, though I left the island with quite a half pint of bastard pearls, sometimes called blisters. These are warts that adhere to the shell and are never a perfect shape, though the colouring in them is quite wonderful. Also in the collection I had a few good small pearls and how I got those is another story and will come in its turn.

Dexter's brother was one grand little entertainer. He usually had something on tap for me and with the help of some of the crew we always put in a pretty full day. One evening he announced that he had sent two boys to the village for dancing girls and we were to meet them on the outer beach, that side of the island facing the ocean. So, leaving the schooner, we paddled to the shore and were soon walking through the coconut groves toward the ocean beach, immediately behind Mrs. Dexter's house. When passing the house, that lady came out on the verandah and said something to Dexter in Tahitian, which of course I did not understand and I must say Dexter looked very sheepish, more so when she repeated her words, with expressions that sounded like an order. Anyhow we kept on going and sure enough, there were the four girls and the two Kanakas[55] men, standing on a level stretch of hard sand. The girls were dressed in long Mother Hubbard wrappers and in these started their dancing, but apparently this was only a sort of warming up process. The boys had gone into the grove and returned with a section of coconut trunk and

---

[55] Name given to natives of South Sea Islands.

several short sticks. Setting the trunk down, they sat beside it and with their sticks started to beat a time which appealed to the ladies, who one by one shed their wrappers, leaving them dressed in the long flowing leaves of Pandanas[56] around their hips, gorgeously dyed in bright colours, with many strings of shells and coral around their necks, pretty much covering their breasts.

The hula-hula has many times been prostituted in American dance halls and on American stages, and many writers have tried to describe it. Both are so far from the real thing that it would be madness for me to go into ecstasy and try my hand at it. First, the reader must remember that the hula-hula belongs to the South Seas, for there it originated and nowhere in the world is its own setting but the South Seas. When staged out-of-doors, stars shining, on a sandy beach where the sea is continually breaking, with the South Sea Trades playing a music among the coconut trees and women dressed in little short of dreams, well, no wonder writers who have seen it have tried to become famous. To my mind every account I have read is damn infamous, it has simply got to be seen to be understood. I saw this dance in Samoa, and of course there we drank the native drink, Kava, and a certain ceremony was gone through in presenting these drinks. No doubt, all this added to the dance. But the hula-hula was not better danced at Samoa than it was by friend Dexter's maidens on Penrhyn.

Sitting down after shedding the wrappers, the ladies started to clap their hands and hit their thighs to the time of the log beating, and worked the muscles of their entire bodies and legs, until suddenly a feeling came over one that there was a sort of wonderful rhythm to all these movements. The whole setting seemed to be in sympathy. The low musical chant of the girls blending with all the

---

[56] Trees characterized by stilt-like aerial roots and the spiral arrangements of their long, graceful, recurved leaves.

noises of nature was marvellous. No, I will not try to explain or describe the hula-hula. It is a wonderful thing to see and nowhere else should it be danced but in the South Sea Islands. There, it is thoroughly understood, and there no possibility of misinterpretation. Girls in that country spend their entire girlhoods learning to dance, even longer than our girls do in the universities, and the real dancer who accomplishes the art to perfection is even more famous, respected and better known than many of our university graduates. The hula-hula dancer[57] of the South Seas is *taboo*, "hands off." She it is who entertains her father's guests, and hospitality thirty years ago in the islands had a meaning all its own. On her shoulders rested her father's honour. If the guest was pleased then certainly the host's family was happy and the family's honour was saved for another day. Of course all girls who danced this dance were not necessarily *taboo*. I don't think Dexter's little friends were. One of the boys asked me to take the sticks and beat time, so of course I sat down at it with a will. Suddenly, the singing stopped and turning around to see the cause, where four girls had a few minutes before been so gracefully dancing in the rays of the night, there stood only one little maid. Boys and girls had all disappeared into the night. Helpless to talk to her and she the same, I got to my feet. I had that day bought from the stores a very bright silk handkerchief. I tied it quickly around her neck, thanked her for the dance and then beat it, yes, actually ran away, in the longest strides I could make, straight for Mrs. Winchester's house. Mrs. Winchester seemed very surprised to see me, but like my lady of the night, she could not talk English so I had nothing to explain. But I do know that she told her husband when he came in a few minutes later where I had been, because he did not ask me where I had been for some time. Of course, I told him the whole

---

[57] "These girls were called *taboos*, and went nowhere unescorted by another woman. At all times their conduct was utterly blameless and chaste," Luxton wrote elsewhere.

115

thing, and he laughed a lot and said he guessed I had taken the wise course. Naturally he told his wife, for a few days later she made me a shirt patterned with bright red roses (I still have it). When she gave it to me she said, as her husband interpreted it, that I was to wear it when she and I went dancing on the outer beach.[58]

Of course Dexter, Pau and the others kidded the life out of me about the silk handkerchief and told me the island chief was going to make me marry the girl. I never did hear the end of that handkerchief during all my stay in Penrhyn. Then Dexter stole my rose-coloured shirt one day when I had it on the line drying, and said he was going to give it to the girl. I chased him overboard, right off the deck of the schooner, and as he was coming up from his dive, I was coming down. I lit right on top of him, knocking every breath out of his body, so he had all he could do to get to the ladder and he was very glad to relinquish the shirt. He really thought I had punched him on purpose and so I would have before I would have gotten in Dutch with Mrs. Winchester.

These fellows were all kidding me because I would not take a wife, such was the custom of the islands. A white man would blow in to see Penrhyn, stay a month or longer, take a wife during his stay and then blow out again. If a baby came along, every one was happy. If it was a boy, every one was very much happier. The baby was a gift from God and so received with joy and feasting. The mother's relatives would fight for ownership, for the real mother never raises her own baby. Why should she? She very likely had quite a number of her sister's babies. No such words as bastard or illegitimate are in the islanders' vocabulary. Living conditions were so easy that family expenses for raising children never entered into the question. Babies

---

[58] It is interesting that Norman Luxton wore this shirt every Banff Indian Days he managed until the last two years when the shirt was practically falling apart from age. It was carefully washed and ironed for the last time and is still kept.

are gifts from the gods and the gods are all nature, so they follow nature without resisting. No woman could be disgraced, because they simply do not look at it that way. Instead she was the envy of her entire family, and only the missionaries might reprove, but what could they do when the entire village applauded so disgraceful a thing with love and joy? Ask yourself.

There was one island I was on for some time when one day the King sent for me. He was in his council house and all his turimen were with him. I could not think of any law I had broken to be summoned before his court. The court had an interpreter and the King asked me if I would care to live on his island. I hesitated for a moment to frame my answer so that I would not hurt his feelings. I certainly had no desire to live on any coral island, but before I could answer he went on to say, "and take one of my daughters?" That was the worst yet. I certainly was in a mess. How was I to get out of it, keep my face clean, and not hurt the dignity and pride of this South Sea Island king? I asked him if he had a map of the Pacific Ocean. He answered that he did not so I sent the interpreter to the *Tilikum* for the chart of the Pacific. When he came back I spread the chart on the table and showed him the course of the *Tilikum*'s sailing, and showed him further where the *Tilikum* intended going. He then asked me where his island was. On a fly-speck south of the equator I placed my finger, and then pointed to America and said it was "Preitane," meaning Britain. He immediately took my pencil and pointed to his fly-speck. He called it Preitane and America his island, nothing so small could be his island. So I let him have his way, my mind was working as to the best way to refuse a princess's hand. There was an old chap with the power of the Czar of Russia, and I might be food for the sharks any minute. He could claim the whole world was his island and I would agree. Then I asked him if Captains Winchester or Dexter ever broke their word to him in the twenty-five years he had known them. He promptly answered that they hadn't, ever.

"All good white men," I said, "keep their word."

"Yes," he said.

"Unless I was a good white man you would not ask me to marry one of your girls?"

"I did not say marry, I said take her," he replied. At this point he got up from his chair and took me to the door of the council hall and from there he pointed to hundreds of coconut trees and told me that they all went with the girl. He sent the interpreter for his girl, and he was not long in coming back. My goodness! There was not one girl but three, so I was quite relieved when the King said I could have my choice, which showed me that I did not have to marry all three. Then we all sat down again, except the girls, who stood up behind their father's chair. Once more I asked the question which he had interrupted to show me the damned coconut trees.

"If I were not a good man you would not ask me to take one of your daughters, would you?" I asked. He admitted perhaps it was so.

"Therefore," I said, "I cannot take one of your daughters, or even marry her, because if I do I will break my word with my comrade Jack Voss, whom I promised to stay with to Australia, and then I would cease to be a good man."

Then here is where I did lie, because I simply could not hurt this old chap's feelings. The ladies' sentiments I did not know.

"But," I said, "when the *Tilikum* voyage is over and if Captains Dexter and Winchester will give me the passage on their beautiful boat, I will return and take one of your daughters." I was a damn fool to add that rider, "and take one of your daughters," for he immediately asked which one I would take. Lordy, oh Lordy! What a fix! I looked the ladies over, or at least I tried to look at them, and asked the interpreter if any had yet been "be-spoke." It seemed that two of them were in a fair way to marriage in the near future, but small obstacles such as that would not stand in the way of any choice I might make. I assured him I would take the one that was free. This pleased the old King and the smallest and the youngest, perhaps fourteen years old, was pointed out to me as the one.

"Take her," said the King, "she is yours." Well, I did not take her and I never went back for her, but I am quite sure that everyone but myself would have been happy if I had taken her that very minute. The King should have been happy after he discovered I did not come back, because I proved myself not a good white man, therefore he was never disappointed at any time, and I hope the little maid was not disappointed, because I was as happy as Hell to get out of such a fix and did not even attend the feast held in honour of my coming nuptials.[59]

---

[59] Although Luxton did refuse one princess, he married another.

IX

Manihiki Island

*A woman's love, leprosy cases. Government of the islands.
Some of the laws. Trying a case. The King and the Judges eat
the fine. Something about Christianity. The gunboat
Torch proves a great teacher. Pulling teeth. The Tilikum is
done over and we leave Penrhyn Island. Manihiki Island
and its wonderful people. Feasting and laughing.
I kiss Jack's girl. Singing all night and dancing.
A real fishing party and eating raw fish.*

Aword or two more about the people of these lagoon islands.
Without a doubt the natives of Penrhyn and Manihiki are
true Maori types. Not only do they speak the Maori language, but they are fierce fighters when necessary, the women quite
as much as the men. Like all brave people they show great strength
in their love and loyalty for their own. This was demonstrated to me
one day when going through the village with Dr. R. S. Bernhard of
H.M.S. *Torch*, looking for leprosy cases. The surgeon found a little

child with this terrible disease, so young that it was still nursing. One thing only could be done. It had to be sent to the Leprosy Island, one of the islands of Penrhyn used to isolate all such cases. This was explained to the mother, who, not hesitating a moment, packed some clothing, picked up her baby, and onto the most lonesome and loathsome islands of all the Pacific she went. Although this mother had no sign of the disease, she was quite willing to sacrifice herself for the love of a child of which she was probably only a foster mother.

It was an ordinary thing to see girls not more than fourteen years old, mothers of children. These child-mothers appeared equally developed as most women would be at twenty or more, and of course equally so at the age of forty or less. All the women took part in the daily labour, boating, sailing, swimming and fishing. They were quite as capable as the men, and in making copra, dried coconut, they were in most cases quicker than the men.

The doctor and I took a trip to the Leprosy Island, and I secured many photos, but unfortunately when getting into the boat I slipped and dropped all the plates into the lagoon. A more desolate, dreary place than this island I was never on. While many of the cases were still alive and active, and a few, like this loving mother, voluntarily there to nurse some loved relative, the majority of the patients sat in their dark little huts all day long, and only one or two had the energy to crawl to the door to take a "look see" at the visitors. One of these was a very grey-headed old lady, with her hair all ragged around her face. She sat in a crouching position with her arms in front of her body and her closed hands on the ground. She had every appearance of a moth-eaten lion. Even the features of her face had taken on a leonine expression. Void of all laughter, singing or dancing, so utterly unlike the two villages of the island, Tautua and Omoka, indeed it was a place to get out of as soon as possible. I think it was the only place in all the South Seas I visited that had no ray of sunshine or happiness. Always in my mind it is the dark spot of an otherwise bright world. The government conditions of both Penrhyn and Manihiki Islands were very similar. There is a king or chief and a yearly election of councillors or turimen, elected by the heads of the homes. There are no written laws, but every so often one of the turimen walking through the village in the evenings bawls at the top of his voice the laws of the islands. Just at the time of our arrival at Penrhyn, some old laws had been rescinded and new ones made. One of the new laws I remember was that everyone could stay out until nine o'clock. Formerly, curfew had been rung at eight, and after nine o'clock you could walk on the beach. For two hours this bawling of the laws disturbed the otherwise wonderful nights. Some of the laws and penalties were: unnecessary Sunday walking fine—five dollars; disagreeing in church with your neighbours—ten dollars; disagreeing in church man and wife—twenty-five dollars; house-breaking of doors or windows—five dollars; theft—twenty-five dollars; card playing—five dollars; dice playing—five dollars; drinking spirits—ten dollars. These were some of the maximum fines.

One case I remember well because the accused was one of the schooner's crew. He got drunk and said he was not. The turiman who caught him said he was drunk, because he smelled liquor on his breath, and without further witnesses for either side the turiman passed the sentence as follows: "Appointed by King Edward the Seventh, I fine you." At this stage the turiman shuts up and the missionary says a prayer for the good of the soul of the accused. Then the turiman goes on. "For getting drunk ten dollars, and for lying twenty-five dollars, and I want you to pay it at once in canned meat and bread" (sea biscuits). The accused sailor proceeded to the store and procured the fine which he carried to the court house. Half was given to the king or chief, and half was given to the turimen present, which happened to be four in this case. Then they all sat down with their families and ate the fine.

I remarked in my diary that on our first entrance to the lagoon I noticed a complete absence of dogs. Captain Winchester told me the reason for this. It seemed that a turiman could sneak around all night, looking for law-breakers, even going into his neighbour's house to find out if he was in bed, and the dogs so often gave the turimen away that in defence of their nightly raids all dogs were banished. Sanitary laws were taken care of by nature, in the shape of low and high tide marks. No outhouses were used. Everyone had to go to the beach and perform the necessary duties below the high tide mark.

A culprit might escape his punishment and be acquitted if he could get possession of the turiman's coat and hat and parade the streets before his trial took place.

It struck me that a lot of these laws were more or less what we might call unethical doings. I would hardly call them even a misdemeanour, let alone a crime, so asking satisfied my curiosity. The missionary was in many cases the directing head. The turimen were more or less his tools, while the chief, or king, was little more than a figurehead.

Outside of singing and dancing the islanders had little enjoyment, and not even checkers were allowed. But to church they must go, five or six times on Sunday, and many prayer meetings during the week. To attend worship it was necessary to dress in European clothes as much as possible, which had a great tendency to overheat the bodies of these children of nature. Colds frequently followed leading to consumption, and of the latter plague I saw quite a lot.

The London Missionary Society operated at both Penrhyn and Manihiki. I met both the reverend gentlemen of these islands. They were natives from some other islands. While they seemed to be well-meaning, they appeared to be all that the laws of the island demanded, and quite in keeping they always wore a dead sort of manner. I never once saw them mingle with the singing or dancing and they always passed such a gathering with a high and mighty expression. Each family subscribed to the church so much a year and paid the missionary's salary. They bought their own Bibles and built their own church. The missionary boat, *Williams* I think it was called, visited all villages every six months and collected presents from the people, besides the tolls already subscribed to the church.

These statements are reminiscences of thirty years ago. Possibly many of the fool laws have changed and possibly more intelligent men are handling government and church affairs. I think it was 1901 or 1902[60] that all the islands were taken under the wing of the different European powers who claimed them, and no doubt they have improved the social conditions.

One day, sitting on the beach at Manihiki beside a native I said to him, "Are you a Christian?"

"Yes," he answered.

"Why are you a Christian?" I then asked him.

"Because," he said, "some day I will be like that," and he pointed to the missionary's boat on the lagoon being rowed by three women. The missionary sat in the stern with an umbrella over his head. He needed it because he was dressed in a clerical cut black suit, a stand-up collar and cuffs, and a black hat. He looked like the hottest thing out of the bad place to me, but still my Manihiki friend envied his clothes, and his soul, for without those soul lights he could never get the clothes.

I had great hopes of my native friend getting his wish because he proved to me that he knew some of his Bible. I was trying to tell him what ice was, and I never went up against anything harder. I explained it every way I could think of, and finally I told him it was hard and thick and that I could walk on it, yes, right across the lagoon. He promptly told me I was a liar, that the only man who ever walked on the water was Jesus Christ. I quit!

The arrival of H.M.S. *Torch* was, of course, one of the big events of the island's history, and while that old gunboat *Torch* was about as

---

[60] *Encyclopedia Britannica*, 1959, XII, 754. These dates are incorrect. Tahiti became a French Protectorate in 1842 and a French Colony in 1877.

prehistoric as Noah's Ark it certainly looked terribly big to the natives. As well as saving Captains Dexter and Winchester a large loss, it embedded into the minds of the natives the might of "Preitane," and the fair and square dealing of the greatest colonizing nation on the globe. Commander Norman J. MacAllister sat for days trying petty native cases, mostly family rows that had no meaning in court. He was always patient and kind, explaining to the parties interested just as a juvenile judge might to his court of children. Some of these complaints, much to the mirth of the whites present, might have happened ten or fifteen years previous to the arrival of the *Torch*. Still, MacAllister would give them sound advice, always to the satisfaction of the natives.

I made friends with all the officers on the *Torch*, and we had many good times together, so I herewith prescribe a list of their names: Commander Norman J. MacAllister, Lieutenant N. Gregory Stapleton, Lieutenant M. F. B. White, Lieutenant Claude Seymour, Surgeon R. S. Bernhard, Engineer E. T. Weeks, Paymaster Hosken, Clerk Hart.

One night I went on board the *Torch* to have dinner and spend the night. This was after the Commander had finished his court at Tautua village and had opened court at Omoka village, the *Torch* having moved outside the lagoon. It came on a good blow, so hard that the old gunboat had to seek wider water, away from the nasty coral reefs. It was several days before we got back, and it was my good fortune to see considerable life on a British gunboat. They were all fine fellows, every one of those officers; of Irish, Scottish and English descent, what else could they be but thoroughbreds?

The surgeon gave me a few pointers in pulling teeth. He also gave me a couple of pairs of forceps to take care of teeth cases, as I might run across them on our trip. Immediately after I had operated on my first tooth my fame ran long and wide on the lagoon. While I never made any charge, all my patients gave me presents, generally in the shape of cat's-eyes, bastard pearls and an occasional real pearl, until I had a good half pint of pretty gewgaws from the lagoon and some real pearls. I remember one old chap coming to the *Tilikum* to have a tooth extracted. He pointed to the tooth that was aching, but to make sure, I probed around with a very fine piece of steel wire I had from my taxidermy kit. I soon found the hole, and the wire disappeared quite half an inch into the tooth. My patient jumped so hard that he displaced the roof boards of the *Tilikum* cabin with his head. The tooth came hard, perhaps through my ignorance, but come it did. The old man thanked me, and departed without the usual present, and certainly I did not blame him. But lo and behold, a few days later he came back with a very beautiful piece of coral, a real pearl, the best I had yet received, and a board about sixteen inches long by four inches wide, beautifully polished with the word *Tilikum* inlaid with mother of pearl shell. He explained to me that the pain in his tooth, before I took it out, had been so great that he often would fight with his wife, but since the tooth was gone he had not beaten her once, so that both of them sent these presents. I could only conclude that I must get paid according to the extent of the pain my patients suffered before the tooth was pulled, and not for the pain I caused in extracting.

All this time I had been tearing around the island shooting, fishing and doing everything but keeping still. Voss was working on the *Tilikum*. He had beached her high up among the coconut trees, emptied everything out of her, scrubbed her clean of mould, even removing the ballast, until she was dry and empty as the day she was first made. The sails and ropes had all gone to pieces, but could be patched, and the hull and decks were void of paint. We had enough money to paint her and some of the canned goods had been saved, so that with coconuts, yams, roots and fish, we could make it very comfortably from island to island.

Time was going and we had been on Penrhyn almost three weeks, so we decided to put to sea once more, but not before we visited Omoka village. This Captain Winchester insisted on, to say good-bye to our friends. Thirty-six hours later we returned to Tautua. There was the *Tilikum* riding at anchor among pearl shell boats, completely new, paint, sails, and ropes. When we boarded her, we found her lockers full of fresh provisions, brands I readily recognized as coming from the island store. Voss was as much mystified as I was. But it was only one guess why Winchester and Dexter had wanted us to go to Omoka, to get us out of the way so those two big-hearted friends Winchester and Dexter, could put a dozen men on the *Tilikum* and make her new.

I could not pay these men, neither could I thank them, I felt positively embarrassed when I tried to tell them my thoughts. Winchester told me to shut up and Dexter grabbed me in his big arms, and all but squeezed the daylights out of me. What could I do but almost cry. They were the finest of the newer Sea Traders, looked down upon by missionaries, like all traders, yet men who taught the natives the real makings of a man and brought prosperity to every island where they did business. To the last of their days I kept in touch with them in Papeete. God rest their souls, for I am sure He has them in his keeping.

Next morning, I think it was about September 20, we raised our anchor. What a farewell. The cheering, crying and presents we received, no one there will ever forget. Warm-hearted, generous kids, just children every one of these islanders, but sail away we must. Dipping our flag to the schooner *Children of Tahiti*, we were soon making fast time across the lagoon to the southwest passage. An hour later the schooner also left, and in two hours' time had passed us. She was certainly a boat to sail.

In thirty-six hours we were under her stern again, with a line from her tied to the *Tilikum*, anchored a short distance from Manihiki[61]

---

[61] One of the Cook Islands or Hervey Archipelago.

and its village. I was not long in getting on board the *Children of Tahiti*, it was like getting back home. How good the coffee tasted, and how good it was to see them all again.

We spent the night on board, and in the morning called on the village. Here I met that famous old pioneer, George Ellis, and his son-in-law, Mr. Williams, who was manager of the trading store owned by Winchester and Dexter. I also met Mr. Hawks, store-keeper of the Pacific Island Trading Company, and Dan, Ellis's son, all of whom were Old Country men excepting Dan. What lore of the Pacific George Ellis could spin, his yarns and experiences were unlimited; what he did not know of this part of the ocean, no one else did. He was one of the very few old time pioneers I met, having come to the South Seas about 1865. For years he lived between Penrhyn and Manihiki, teaching the natives all he knew of the sea, boats and sails, until to this day these islands are a standard that all other lagoon islands follow as a pattern in sailing, fishing, boat-building, cultivation of coconuts and copra. Ellis had a wonderful collection of worn-out books and writings, reminiscences of trips he had taken, short and incomplete logs, none of which I could make head nor tail of, but he could always fill in every detail. Everyone called him a "damn liar," perhaps he was, but to my mind he was the man who had blazed the trail for others to follow. Certainly the natives were years ahead of their time in prosperity by his early arrival and teachings.

No island in the Pacific ever could equal Manihiki in its hospitality. From the early morning when we stepped on shore until the sun set it was one continual round of dinners. The first meal I sat down to I naturally thought would be the last until lunch. So it was, but lunch was a continuation of the others, and so on. Every half hour or hour it was announced that the next meal would be at so and so's. Family after family tried to outdo themselves in feeding us. I forgot our many hostesses' names in the mass of native foods we ate and smelled for days after. They could cook. That first dinner I could never forget; Mr. Williams's native wife, Tira, and her friend Koteka, wife of Loapa, cooked it. They put coconuts up in a dozen different ways. With yams it was a hundred ways, and with fish from the lagoon and chicken, pig and taro,[62] it was a menu that would make a French chef die of envy. All day, yes, all day we ate, I can't say feasted, because by half past ten I was so full I could hardly move and by six I refused to move. Family after family brought in its dinner and at it we would go, tasting a little here and a little there. All this as they told me was to show their appreciation of our calling at Manihiki.

Apparently our fame had gone before us for I was asked why our boat carried dead men's heads in her hold. This was sort of a knock-out as I had no idea that they knew I had Siwash skulls in the *Tilikum*'s hold. I told them I was a collector of all things, and these skulls were so old that no one felt badly about me carrying them away from their graves. I sent one of the *Children of Tahiti* crew to the *Tilikum* for some of the skulls, and during the afternoon I explained to the diners the reason for the shapes of the skulls. How these foolish old mothers would tie a small piece of wood to a wee baby's head and leave it there to make the skull grow into any fantastic shape that she might have in mind. It was, it seemed to me, hours that they kept me talking of the Americana (Indians), trading posts, snow, ice, furs, buffalo and dog-trains. Perhaps it was a line of talk they had never heard before. They were deeply interested and some days afterwards the King kept me for a good half day going into more details of the Canadian North West, the mountains and the Pacific Coast. He was "Apollo" Arika, a man about forty-five years old who looked sixty. King of Manihiki, he was a really agreeable chap, perhaps because he had nothing else to do but be agreeable. He never

---

[62] Plants of the arum family grown throughout the tropics for their edible starchy tuberous rootstock.

worked, he got half of all the fines his turimen collected and he had only one wife. She put up a very fine dinner for us even though we had eaten all day at the Council Hall. I am sure it was a good dinner from what all my native friends said, and also from the size of their extended fronts. Beyond that I do not know because I simply could not eat any more. At the King's dinner girls kept coming in and putting Pandanas hats, beautifully made from fine stripped Pandanas leaves, on Voss's head and mine. Hat after hat, one on top of the other, until the whole stack would fall off our heads. Then another stack would start, until they were so high that the donators would have to stand on a stool to put a hat on to the pile. It was quite a while before I was informed that all these hats were being taken to the *Tilikum*. The hats were ours and should be put on our boat, that was the native version. I did not want the hats and I knew the store gave two or three shillings for each one. Why take these presents? To head off this spontaneous gift giving I told them a story of a custom in Canada, only I called Canada "Preitane."

In Preitane, I said, if a girl puts her hat on a man's head, it is an invitation for the man to kiss her. I naturally thought the hat giving business would quit, but not so. Along down the aisles between the tables came a very old woman and one of the very few rather pretty girls I had seen in the islands. Her name, I think, was Kina, meaning "beautiful sunlight and shadows." Each carried a hat. The old lady went to Voss and put her hat on his head, and I can still see her standing there acting like something about sweet sixteen that had never been kissed. Had she not been promised one? That damned old Viking sat there pushing the yams and coconut tarts down his throat as if no one else was on earth. I yelled at him, "Buss her, Jack," but all he did was lick his fingers and pull the hat more to his liking with his dirty paws. By this time Kina had put her hat on my head. She was a wee thing of only eighty pounds, so I whipped off my seat, picked her up bodily, sure, and kissed her so they all could see. I then carried her over to Voss, and while I held his head she kissed him. Then I saluted the old lady as well, and the natives howled their applause. Voss spoke lots of times afterwards about Manihiki. It was one of the islands he said he did not like because of these natives. They were no different than many other natives I met in other lands. They liked a joke and they liked to give one, but they wanted their jokes received in the same manner in which they received yours. Otherwise you might as well go home, your fun was finished at that party. And so it was for Voss as long as we stayed on that island.

Kissing is not a general expression throughout the islands and many islanders resent it. It is usual to rub noses with the women and shake hands with the men. The women generally smell strongly of coconut oil which is almost as offensive as our perfumed ladies of America.

Mr. and Mrs. Williams were mighty good to us while we stayed at Manihiki. His house was ours and we ate as we liked, for Mrs. Williams was always ready to give us a bite or a cup of coffee. Speaking of coffee, let me tell you how all these islanders cooked coffee. The green bean was taken and roasted, immediately ground and put into a small strainer. This was held over the coffee cup and the boiling water poured through it. The liquid was as black as ink, and in a week or ten days I acquired such a craving for this wonderful drink that it frightened me. I cut it out, using green coconuts instead. Coffee was served to us about ten times a day when we were aboard the *Children of Tahiti*, and I got so I was looking for it and would get quite grouchy if I happened to miss it. It was a desire I never had for liquor. Certainly, it was time to cut it out, and I did since I was getting as nervous as a cat.

The natives on this island were even more musical than at Penrhyn and the law about going to bed at nine o'clock was not so rigidly enforced. Every evening we would sit on the Williams's verandah and listen to melodies quite equal to that of the Southern darkies. Here, Jack said he heard songs he had not thought of since he left Denmark, and I heard all the old college songs and every popular air ever composed. Certain natives, sailing on the trading schooners, made it their business never to come back to an island without bringing a new song. This was always done by word of mouth and the memory for the air by ear. In no time these islanders knew hundreds of songs. For hours we would sit and listen and only regret that the nights were not longer. One of the best song carriers happened to be on the island when we were there. This man really had an ear for music. He had the different voices all classified and each voice came in, in its turn, or all together as his baton instructed. He was certainly good. He was an ugly little man and one of the smallest that I had seen on the island, but when you looked at him, after hearing him sing, all you could think of was that wonderful, sweet, tenor voice. You soon forgot all about his features. It was like what someone said of Lavina of Tahiti. "Dear sweet old Lavina, your arms are like legs of mutton, it is true your breasts are huge like cabbages, but we never saw those things, we just saw you as a good, sweet woman." I think it was MacQuarrie,[63] in *Tahiti Days*, who said that, and it was so true. There is something in all these islands that gets the average white man. Deformities are lost sight of in the tremendous joy of just living among a race of people so happy and contented, and Manihiki natives all struck me that way. Their village was really clean. This, I discovered, came from George Ellis's teachings, and the road through the coconut groves that led to the other village, Tukao, was defined by clean fine white coral spread several inches deep.

Several times during my stay at Penrhyn and Manihiki Islands I asked to go fishing, and while Captain Dexter's brother was always ready to meet me a hundred percent on any of my suggestions, he told me that to fish in the daytime was a waste of time. I could hardly

---

[63] Hector MacQuarrie, *Tahiti Days* (New York: G. H. Doran Co., 1920), Illus.

credit such a statement because I had seen fish in the bottom of the lagoon by the tens of thousands. A very few fish could be enticed to your hook during the day, and what strange hooks they were that the natives used. It was a piece of pearl shell about four inches long by half an inch wide, with a hole in one end for the line. The part that the fish took was another piece of pearl shell, sharp and hook-shaped, tied to the other end of the piece of shell with a piece of red cotton for bait. Some of the fish took this cunning lure, but to get them in the daytime the fisherman had to go to the passage-way leading from the lagoon to the ocean. Here there was always more or less of a rip tide or wind, so that such work as this involved did not appeal to the native. Instead, he knew that at any time he could get all the fish he required by waiting for the fall of night, when with a net or spear, in a few minutes, by walking along the shallow waters of the lagoon beach, he could fill his wife's and daughter's baskets to capacity.

One day Dexter said, "Tonight I will show you fishing that you will never forget." Although I never wrote one word of that night's fishing in my diary, as he said, I never did forget. The moon must have been full because I saw its light on the water. The coconut trees looked three times higher than they really were. Noises of talking, "Where is my net?" "Where are those baskets?" and, "My spears" were all that could be heard for a while. All the time the crowd of natives was collecting on the lagoon shore, so that when the policemen of the village, eight in number, finally gave the word to begin, I am sure there must have been four hundred men and women on the beach with nets, spears, baskets, coconut torches and gaffs. What a sight it was! Quite seventy-five carried torches of inflammable leaves and baskets, also made of leaves, four to five feet long and shaped like a cigar. The rest were fishermen and fisher-women. Stretched out along the shore the line reached easily a quarter of a mile. Torches, fishing baskets, spears and nets were all intermingled with each other. At the word, the extreme end of the line waded into the lagoon. The end man was almost waist weep. Then they all advanced following the shore line, and here is where the fun started. In no time the baskets were filled. Young boys and girls carried empty baskets to the basket carriers in the lagoon, and carried back the baskets full of fish, spilling them into piles all along the shore. Torch-lights, moon, cries of excitement, never drowned the singing that was going on all the time by the leading line of the fish patrol. Such a sight is beyond description. Fish by the thousands came to the light of the torches, and were caught in nets on the ends of poles and spears. Never in all my life did I ever see so many fish, not only so many fish, but so many different colours and shapes of which I never dreamed anything in the sea could take. A wonderful bed of pansies or African daisies had nothing on these fish for colours. One, a perfectly red thing about the same as a two pound trout, was poison to eat. Still another, the colour of ink, was considered something to be prized. Another that looked like a human skull, without the cross-bones, was not a favourite. The fishing lasted perhaps three-quarters of an hour and I am quite sure there were two or three tons of fish on the beach. There was no such thing as dividing the piles. Everyone helped himself, until there were only comparatively few of the undesirable fish left to be carried away at high tide to feed their fellows. I saw Dexter select with care some dozen fish that looked very much like our small whitefish of northern Canada, telling me that we would have a feed of real fish.

Late that night we sat down to a fish dinner, with yams and coffee, that was simply delicious. And when Dexter told me I had been eating raw fish, I would not credit his statement. He proved it by going to the cook's galley. He took one of these fish, squeezed two limes on it, and asked me to try it. It was absolutely the same as I had been eating.

Can anyone imagine such a fishing party, with moonlight, coconut trees, water and the South Sea Trades blowing the water into phosphorescent lights. Four hundred grown-up children sang songs, with a melody beyond description. The scene was illuminated by torches that would go out, only to come on again with service supplied by the younger element. No wonder there are beachcombers in the South Sea Islands who will never go home.

X

Samoa

An island wedding. Leaving our friends.
Danger Island and on to Samoa. Jack and I have a
showdown as to who is boss. Samoa from the sea.
A picture worth seeing. A word on the Samoans.
The making and drinking of Kava and an evening
entertainment. Morals of the natives.
A lady of large legs and breasts.

We stayed on Manihiki and a most peaceable time I had. Jack slept on board the *Tilikum*. There was no passage to the lagoon from the ocean to get the canoe in, and it was not safe to anchor outside without a watch. We visited Tukao village several times seeing Mr. Hawk, Mr. Williams, Dan and George Ellis and we always received a wonderful welcome. The dinners were fabulous! We had whole, roasted, little pigs fed on milk coconuts and no one would touch anything until Jack and I had been served. So it was with every dish. We took first choice and the devil got the hindmost. I came to love and respect those women like my own. Not that they were pretty. I never saw a pretty South Sea Island lady, but Hell, man, they would mother you and feed you until you would have to yell for help.

My diary says, "Tuesday, September 24th," it was one forty-five a.m. when I lay down on the verandah to go to sleep, but it was two hours before I managed it. All that singing going through my mind and wee tots three to ten years old, by the dozens, dancing. They can do it almost as well as the grown-ups. What a life it would be if the islands were only larger.

Wednesday, September 25th, every yard of cotton and print had been bought at the store. A raised seat had been built among the trees, and from the bride's house to the seat these yards of prints, all colours, were spread along the ground. There was going to be a wedding and everyone donated, even the pigs and chickens squealed, but not in delight. I hunted up the bridegroom. He was a poor delicate man, consumptive I am sure, and his bride so fat and happy. I asked him what he was going to wear to his wedding and he said a "lava-lava" which is about two yards of print tied around the hips and thighs. "Not good enough," I replied. I took him aboard the *Tilikum* and dressed him in a blue serge suit, white shirt with collar and cuffs, socks, pumps and a broken derby. I also gave him a swagger stick. The whole outfit was much the worse for mildew, but Mrs. Winchester had made them look pretty nice. The groom thought it was all right anyway as he said, "Just like missionary." It certainly was and I bet hot too. He cut a great figure among his island friends and it was easily seen that his bride was very proud of him. That wedding was something like our feast, for it lasted all day and all night and was still going strong when we sailed away Thursday morning. After we got out of sight of the island we threw overboard dozens of nuts, cooked meats, yams and other foods, as well as dozens of hats, simply to make room to get around in the canoe. The canoe was one mass of Pandanas leaves tied to everything imaginable, and the masts could not be seen for them. Yes, Manihiki was a lovely place to visit. It was just one big piece of hospitality.

A little incident happened just before we left. I tried to pull up the anchor which Jack had let go that morning when we breakfasted on the *Children of Tahiti*, but he had fouled it in the coral and I could not budge it. I could see it quite plainly on the bottom in the coral so overboard I went, following the anchor rope. I just got my hand on the ring of the anchor when I suddenly discovered I wanted air worse than I had ever wanted coffee. I thought I would never get to the surface and finally, when I did bob up, I was so played out that I had to be pulled on deck, where I stretched and gasped for a good three minutes. King Apollo was there with his two daughters to see us off. He said something to one of the men in his boat and immediately I heard a splash. He had gone after the anchor. What do you suppose he did? Not only did he free the anchor, but he put it on his shoulder and brought it to the surface. It weighed about thirty-five pounds.

It was about three hundred miles to Danger Islands, our next intended stop, taking three days on account of very light winds. On the third day we came in sight of the islands. Not knowing much about the coast, nor where to anchor, we hove to for the night. Next morning we steered for the palms and soon uncovered three islands, all joined apparently by water-breaking reefs. We saw the village and shaped our course accordingly to get to it. I kept sounding the depth as Jack steered and found deep water immediately up to the beach. Throwing the anchor out to the natives, who by this time had come to meet us, the *Tilikum* took up the slack, the wind keeping her nicely from bumping the shore.

We had no desire to stay long at Danger Islands, and it was only the urgent asking of the chief that persuaded us to stay some three hours. Like the other islands, they wanted to feast and entertain us. I assured them Jack and I were so full from eating at Manihiki that it would be several days yet before we dared eat more. The chief laughed and said, "Manihiki man good man." Still, he brought us some beautiful young, green coconuts, a couple of cooked chickens and a leg of young pig. We thanked him for all his good presents and headed the old war canoe for Samoa, which was about four hundred miles away. We made it in three days.

The wind blew those three days in a quarter very favourable to the *Tilikum*. Each of my watches when Jack would go to sleep, I would tie all the clothes I could find to the stays and masts, in order that we would make more mileage per day, and get to land that much sooner. I never disrobed the rigging until Jack had taken the tiller or helm, for I was not trying to put anything over that I did not wish him to know. With a pair of pants, a coat and a shirt or two so hung on the stays, I reckoned the canoe was good for five to eight miles more in each of my two six-hour watches in the twenty-four hours. The second morning out, the old cedar log was certainly tearing the miles off, and the way it leaped from the top of each wave made Jack Voss hang on to his pots and kettles when he was cooking breakfast. Steering a boat in a wind like this you are plumb foolish to ever take your eyes off the front of your boat or compass. There comes a feeling to you, as each wave rides past the bottom of the boat, that tells just what way to port or starboard your helm should go to ride the next wave without danger. I was very intent on this job when with a roar like an animal, Jack grabbed the back of my neck, actually tearing my shirt partly off, and shot me head first into the hatchway of the cabin. I suppose he must have immediately taken the steering stick else the canoe would have come to grief. Partly stunned, I picked myself up, not seriously hurt, and drank several cups of coffee. While I was doing this, Voss told me I would sail the boat the way he wanted or else he would kill me, saying that he could easily throw me overboard and report me as missing at his next port of call. He said much more that I did not hear, or else have forgotten, all that went through my mind was, "throw me overboard," and physically fit as he was, he could do it easily. All through the last six thousand miles this vile temper of his had been getting worse and worse. If I now buckled down to it, my life would be worse than any dog's that he might have owned, and while drinking the coffee I thought it all out. It had to be one of us for the sea and fishes. One boss, and I would be that boss in just another five minutes. I took my time, ate a good meal of young pig, bread and more coffee, and washed up the dishes. Then I went forward to the small locker that reached out on the foredeck from inside the cabin. Here I kept medicine, camera, plates and all the ammunition for the guns. Putting all the ammunition into a sack, I picked up the twenty-two long-target Stevens pistol. Loading it, I stepped out of the cabin hatch and forward to the main mast, there dropping the bag of bullets and shells on the roof of the cabin. I presented the gun at Jack's head, telling him to beat it below faster than he had ever gone in his life. Otherwise, I told him, I'd shoot him dead and wouldn't report him as missing either, but as a damned pirate that I had to kill to save my own life. I told him to go and to go fast, and Jack went and went fast. Then, kicking the top of the hatch shut with my foot, I had hold of the steering stick two seconds after Voss had left it. I knew every move I was going to make. Coffee, young pig and rough treatment are great thinking matters. I told Jack to throw me out a padlock, and I also told him where to find a clasp and hasp, and instructed him to put them on the hatch cover so that it would lock with the pull-up hatch that led into the cabin from the cockpit. Jack did everything I told him to do, and there was not one word of excuse or trying to square his rough treatment. I locked the cabin hatch that afternoon about three p.m. The fresh breeze had died down a lot and, by tying the tiller, the old canoe steered herself. If not, the main boom would let me know when the canoe came up into the wind by tapping me on the head. I slept for four hours, and when I wakened the *Tilikum* was going on the same course as I had set her on when I went to sleep. When I unlocked the cabin hatch Jack passed out the meal he had already cooked. That night I sighted land and told Jack so, but I also told him to keep his feet on the cabin floor. If I had not trusted him before I certainly did not now, that is, as far as personal contact might be concerned. He wasn't any more sure of where Apia, the port of Samoa, was, than I. So, playing the old game, I hove to, hung up a lantern on the main mast, locked Voss in the cabin, threw out the anchor, and went to sleep. Day was breaking when I awoke, and going forward I pulled in the anchor, then unlocked the cabin and told Voss to make Apia harbour, which was quite clearly seen on the shore line.

It was indeed a beautiful sight that morning looking at Samoa, clear cut in the deep tropical colours of foliage on the sides and hills of the island, with cultivated areas of many descriptions. The houses and buildings stood out wonderfully sharp in the morning light. It was not any trouble to make the harbour, and we anchored a few yards from the shore to await the coming of the port master, customs officer and medical inspector. Voss asked me what I was going to do with him. I told him that we would have to have a thorough understanding that would preclude more rows. That was the end of it for the time being.

Soon Mr. Burkheim, the customs officer, came on board and when he heard that we were from Vancouver Island he could hardly credit our statement. He was very nice to us, clearing us of all port or harbour expenses. Mr. Reinhardt, also of the customs, told us to tie our boat up to the government wharf, where a wharf policeman would watch it night and day. This we did, but not before he warned us very particularly about guns, and not for any reason to take them on shore as all guns on the island had been confiscated by the German government after a recent native uprising. We then went ashore where I stayed at a hotel called, I think, the "International" run by Robert Hiscock. I didn't see Voss again until the morning I decided to clear for the Fiji Islands.

I met a Mr. King, an American traveller, Mr. Wagenberg and Captain Seymour and Mr. Swan, an English chemist, all within a few minutes of landing. The latter two I spent many happy days with, visiting the interior of the island and native villages.

It was not long before I discovered that Samoan natives hate work and unless compelled to do so, never will. But they play cards, chess, checkers, dance, sing, swim, canoe and drink Kava. Yes, they will do it the twenty-four hours around, and then some. They also had a business that is not at all hard in so far as manual labour was concerned. They were just as keen after the tourists trying to sell them souvenirs, as salesmen at Niagara Falls. That was thirty years ago, so that today they must, I am sure, have the souvenir sellers of America licked off the map. Indeed, they were very different to my Penrhyn and Manihiki friends. The women were better looking, even though darker, and all carried themselves with wonderful poise. It was pleasing to look at them, either walking or dancing. They never tired or lost the grace of their motions. They could also make Kava that made our legs so drunk we had to stay with our host all night, whether we wished to or not, to awaken in the morning and find one of the daughters of the house fanning us to keep the flies away. The hula-hula here was quite as interesting as the version danced on the islands we had come from, but the Kava drinking was new so I must tell of it.

Captain Seymour was my guide on this occasion. We were in a big hut, where all of forty natives were present, all sitting on our butts around the wall of the hut. Two girls came in carrying a large wooden bowl with more than four legs on it. Setting the bowl on the floor, they passed among us, opening their mouths to show us the insides and teeth pointing out how clean they were. Then, taking a piece of wood, which is the root of the Kava plant and belongs to the pepper family, they put several sections of it into their mouths and commenced chewing and spitting. They kept this up for several minutes until the cud of the chewing was quite dry and the juices were exhausted. They then filled the bowl with clear drinking water, casting into it the dry cuds from their mouths. Then, scattering the chewed fabrics of root through the water, they gathered it together again with their hands and squeezed it. This was repeated many times until I was quite sure their hands must be very clean. After the last time of squeezing, the bowl was absolutely cleared of the fibre. There was milky fluid left, thus the Kava. The head *taupo*[64] girl then took a coconut shell cup, and dipping from the bowl filled the cup full of the liquid. She presented it with graceful, bowing movements to the guest of honour. If the guest is on his job he will try to gulp it all without a swallow, letting it run down his gullet. Then, instead of giving the cup back to the *taupo*, he throws it with all his might at the centre post of the hut. If he hits, the cup shatters into a hundred pieces and the crowd all yells. But if he misses, someone yells that he was hit instead of the post. So the evening went on all night long. They danced, sang and drank Kava, and he is a poor fish that can't enjoy such music though the women's bodies stink of coconut oil. Sometimes, to break the program, a prize of a handkerchief or a few yards of cloth was tied high up the centre pole of the hut. This pole was as smooth as glass, but when greased it was like smooth ice. It was greased from some ten feet above the ground up to whatever was tied to the pole. Then in came a young or an old man. The prize on the pole was pointed out to him, and he was told that it was his if he could get it. Of course, he tried, doing fine until he reached the

---

[64] *The World and Its Peoples, Australia-New Zealand-Oceania* (New York: Greystone Press, 1966), p. 186. "The *taupo* is a young maiden, chosen from among noble families to become village or tribal mistress of ceremonies. She is the most important person during the traditional courtesy visits known as *malaga*, frequently made between villages. The *taupo* greets the most important guests; she does not enjoy the liberty enjoyed by girls of her own age, always being accompanied by at least one lady in waiting; and her behaviour must always be controlled and blameless."

grease. Then, down the pole he slid only to be smacked on his bare butt by the girls using a flat stick and from the sound and from the manner in which the would-be prize getter moved up the pole, it must have hurt. Down he slid again, and in desperation broke for the door, only to be grabbed by the crowd. On their hands above their heads, he was moved so quickly around the circle that he looked more like a barrel with legs and arms on it than a human being. It was rather rough play but all seemed to enjoy it, even the goat.

Sometimes, someone wished to go out to relieve himself, and man or woman on his return took hold of his ankle and stopped him. Someone else would say, "Whose son are you?" He, of course, answered them by giving his father's name. "Why did you go out of the singing just now?" He told them. "Did you have a good passage?" Perhaps by this time he would tire of the silly questions, though all in fun, and try to move on. That was the signal, for he was then grabbed and passed around the circle on the hands and arms held above the sitting heads, and how rough they played it their bodies showed them the next day.

It was this utter lack of decency that I could never get used to, and such language was pretty general throughout the islands. Although most of the natives professed Christianity, they never thought that foul words and thoughts might hurt their spiritual character. It was simple indeed when you understood their point of view. In no manner of action or thought were there such words as immoral or indecent, not, at least, in the meaning of the words as we take them. Nature was the most natural thing to them and if it came up for discussion it came up in all its minuteness and glaring ugliness, as it would seem to us, but not to them.

I saw quite a lot of Samoan natives, and I admired their grace and happy manner of living. They were far more indolent than the lagoon folks and even seemed to have fewer cares than my other friends of the small, flat islands.

It was a week or more after our stay in Apia that I wished to buy a pair of shoes. Crossing the road to a large store that would be large even in a place of fifty thousand population in Canada, I found what I required. I told the native clerk that I would take them but on offering him the dollar or so, the price marked, he refused the money informing me that the shoes were a present from the proprietor of the store, given to so brave a man who was not afraid of the winds and waves of the Pacific. I hesitated about accepting the present. I had not met the owners of this business, and they certainly owed me nothing. Just then Mr. Swan, the English chemist, came in and I explained my predicament to him. However, he assured me in a laughing manner that it was quite all right to accept the shoes. After he had made his purchases we adjourned to his place of pills and had some drinks of real Scotch which he always had a standing order for from the mail boat arriving from Sydney.

It was in the evening, along about dark, when a wee native boy handed me a note, waiting until I read it. The note was written quite childishly but plainly, requesting me to follow the boy and receive some entertainment, possibly much to my profit and enjoyment. It was quaintly written in words apparently of much choosing. Throwing away the good cigar that was all but consumed, I followed my little guide across the street and up a stairway on the side of the store building where I had received the present of shoes that afternoon. There he left me at the head of the stairs and a native girl escorted me down a long, well carpeted hall to the front of the building. Opening the door, she asked me to enter. It was a much larger room than I expected, beautifully furnished and the walls were covered with many relics of the South Seas. I immediately wanted to examine and study the collection, but never was such a pleasure afforded. A voice called from a door at the farthest corner end of the room, "Normie, Normie, is that you, Normie?" I always hated Normie, but nevertheless I answered.

"Yes, it is Luxton."

"Come, come quickly," was the reply, "this girl will surely kill me."

Moving across the large sitting room to the door, I passed in and there, lying on a large bed, was a counterpart of MacQuarrie's "Lavina" of *Tahiti Days*. "Dear sweet Lavina, your arms were like legs of mutton, it is true your breasts were huge like cabbages." But I wish to goodness MacQuarrie could have been present to have described these members which were reclining on the side of the bed, while a native girl was being strapped, apparently for rough rubbing of the same members. And all the time this punishment was being administered, the damsel was calling me. "Come, come quick, and show this bad girl how a lady's leg should be treated." Now what the devil would you have done? I am sure her legs were quite as large as any case of elephantiasis I had ever seen, but the "cabbages" and "legs of mutton" in plain view proved she was not suffering from any such disease. On the contrary, everything was quite symmetrical, even to a huge tub of ice that must have come off the mail steamer that afternoon, and a pretty price it must have cost, I'll swear. All the ice was interlaced with champagne and brands of Scotch that I had not seen since leaving the Canadian shores. All this wonderful hospitality and a lady's leg to be rubbed. So far, old Jack Voss and I had got past with fairly good success all pleasures offered, but to handle this case was quite beyond any experience I had yet gone through. Asking this much exasperated lady what the trouble might be, she informed me that she had slipped and strained her knee. Then, to prove her assertions, much to the consternation of myself and the bed which groaned under every move she made, she showed me the other knee. To save my soul I could not see one bit of difference between the two of them. They were quite the largest I had ever seen, outside of "Jumbo's," the largest lady elephant Barnum's Circus ever owned. She insisted that I rub her knee. Equally insistent, I tried to tell her of my rough hands from rope pulling, salt water and coral. Then, noticing that she was using a lotion of oil, I assured her such a soft fluid would never penetrate deep enough to ease the strained muscles of the knee, and that I had on board the *Tilikum* a very much valued remedy used by the American Indians that would without doubt cure all ills. Very reluctantly she gave me her consent to depart to get this medicine, telling me she knew I would never return, that always being the case. Did I forget to say this lady was of dark complexion? Well, she was. Not Samoan, but from my dear island Manihiki. She had married a Scandinavian captain, owner of a whaler whose ship had not so very long before this been wrecked. The lady of his choice had actually saved his life. With the insurance from his boat he built up a general store business in Apia which was a credit to that Pacific port. But, poor fellow, he was called long before expected, leaving his business to a "child," his widow, and some haphazard natives, whose brains should have been considerably more keen in order to have classified them as managers. It seemed it was this lady's ambition to find a manager for this business and, as Swan told me, the methods used with me were the usual procedures she employed in getting acquainted with any likely looking prospect that might hit the beach of Apia. I didn't see this lady of the elephantine legs again until the morning we left Apia harbour. It was early in the morning and a nasty breeze was blowing, but my dear and very large lady was there to wish us Godspeed. Like her relatives of Manihiki she loaded us down with presents. In that moment I almost believed MacQuarrie, and might even have rubbed her knee if I had not been in such a hurry. There was a real something on the wind and it was up to us to clear to a wide sea or be stayed up in Apia.

It was years after in the village of Banff, the Canadian Playground of the Rockies, that I met one of those kindred spirits always looking to see "what was on the other side of the hill," who told me the end of this lady. It seems that she was at last successful in securing a manager for her store. On just what basis this business agreement was decided he did not know, nor was he sure of this white man's nationality. Of one thing he was certain. The large business soon went into the hands of creditors, and on a small island somewhere in the Pacific what was saved of the wreck, a small trading store, was opened only to last a short time. My lady of the large legs, discovering that her spouse was seeking enjoyment of the island women, one night broke his head in with a weapon of her own choosing, and finished by committing her huge body to the sea.

XI

Suva

A visit to Robert Louis Stevenson's home. Samoa a place to live.
Leaving Samoa, an understanding with Jack. Storms,
but seek relief under a volcanic island. A blustering chief
and Jack shoots up the natives. A collection of curios.
Jack's uncanny reckoning. I wreck the Tilikum. Picked up
for dead. More human skulls. Many wrecks through these
islands. Suva and I pass out. Secure mate for Voss.
Kindness of a steamer captain. Meet again in Sydney.
Voss's terrible experience.

Anyone who would visit Apia and not cross the island hasn't seen why the Samoan has no need to work. From trees or bush as our hunger called Mr. Swan and I took as we desired, and at night a friendly native village was always close to receive us and entertain with Kava and the hula-hula, or siva-siva, as the dance is called in Samoa.

149

Do not miss the Sliding Rock and lakes on the journey. What wonderful water Samoa has. No one but a lagoon island hunter will ever appreciate it fully. Little wonder that at Sliding Rock I stayed until Swan threatened to leave me.

Robert Louis Stevenson, best read of all fiction writers of the South Seas, here had his home and last resting place. I stood in awe in the shade of the palms, glimpsing through the foliage those broad verandahs that once sheltered this great man. "Vailima" was the name of it, and far up behind it were the steep slopes of a mountain on the top of which rest the last mortal remains of the greatest friend that the Samoan natives ever had. As long as the Roman roads in the path of that great nation will last, so long will the memory of Robert Louis Stevenson's name remain in Samoa.

The wonderful story of this man's burial has no place in these pages of the *Tilikum*, but those who wish to read that story will not have far to go. I'd simply like to repeat the memorial inscription written by the tenant of the tomb himself, and placed there by his friends after his death. It is a complete and satisfactory answer to my not all morbid curiosity.

Under the wide and starry sky,
Dig the grave and let me lie.
Glad did I live and gladly die,
And I lay me down with a will.

This be the verse you grave for me:
Here he lies where he longed to be;
Home is the sailor, home from the sea,
And the hunter home from the hill.

I think it must have been about the 9th of October that I hunted Jack Voss up, and suggested that we should be moving on. The next morning before daybreak I took Voss to Mr. Swan's store and read to him an account of our differences while on the voyage, with a full statement of what he threatened to do to me if I refused to sail the boat in the manner in which he wished, and that if at our different ports of call between Samoa and Australia I did not appear with the *Tilikum*, Mr. Swan was to take such action as he saw fit to make Voss prove to him that violence had not been the cause of my disappearance. This paper Voss signed as correct, and as a true statement of what had passed between us. A few friends were down at the canoe to see us off. Storm signals were flying from the government flag poles and all small fishing boats outside the harbour were making all sail to reach its inside barriers. However, in spite of all this the *Tilikum* cleared the harbour entrance. Then for three days she experienced the most difficult of all weather during her short runs. For three days we didn't get a glimpse of the sun, and it was only because of Voss's uncanny dead-reckoning, in which I had every faith, that we pretty well knew where we were. The 12th of October late at night we smelled land, and in a few hours we were out of raging storms and in the lee of an island. Although we could see nothing of it we knew it was there. Next morning, there it was sure enough. Niuafo'ou, part of the Tonga group. A friendly fishing boat took me ashore but I soon discovered that the village was on the other side of the island. I returned to the *Tilikum* and again went back to the island. Each time this meant climbing a good high cliff since the harbour as well as the village was on the other side of the island. Also, a white man lived some three miles away from the anchorage. I had hardly covered a mile when I met him on horseback. His name was Mr. C. C. Flower, and he seemed to be worried by our presence on the island. Although I tried to tell him we were storm bound, he insisted that we should have a permit from the Tonga Island government. Later, the chief assured me that the natives were not at all friendly to strange white folks, and a piece of "long pig"[65] was very tempting to their still unsatisfied craving. It was only a few years after the missionary and his assistants had all disappeared. This chief, Folofile, was anything but a friendly beggar and blew hard of what an all-powerful chief he was. It seemed that years in the past Niuafo'ou had captured Tonga, some three hundred miles distant. All this talk with the chief was most unsatisfactory to Mr. Flower, so I told him I would go back to the *Tilikum*. I also assured the chief that if he called on me I could make more noise than he could. So after drinking some Kava with Mr. Flower at his house, I departed for the canoe and got aboard at four p.m. I told Jack of my visit and of the man-eating history of the natives, and as much as Jack hated to do it he stayed up all night in the lee of the island as it was blowing a real gale. He preferred to stay on watch all night himself, and to satisfy his nerves I loaded all the guns and sprinkled the roof of the cabin and the foredeck with carpet tacks that old George Ellis insisted on me taking along when he heard that we were going to the Fiji Islands. These tacks had an extra large flat head with a short shaft, so that when dropped they invariably stood with the business end up. Ellis had them made long ago to repel boarders.

It was just getting light the next morning when I was roused out of a sound sleep by the darndest bang I had yet heard aboard the *Tilikum*. Rushing out of the bunk up the hatch and onto the roof of the cabin, I promptly stepped on just about one million tacks. Certainly I swore and swore good while getting the tacks out of my feet. I saw Jack gazing off toward the island and, looking that way, I could see about two hundred and fifty yards distant some twenty catamarans,[66] all empty. Jack told me when he came aft that the natives had been lowering their catamarans all night over the cliff.

---

[65] Human flesh as prepared for a feast by cannibals: so called from a Maori and Polynesian term.

[66] Two canoes fastened side by side, making a raft.

They apparently had carried them two miles across the island for only one reason Jack could see. He waited for them to get in mass formation and close enough. Then he trained the cannon on them and fired. Every one of the natives went overboard and out of sight, like so many Hell-diving ducks. Jack had not known that I had unshipped the cannon at Apia and had neglected to make it fast again. The result was that the recoil of the black powder kicked the gun from the block and, before Jack realized it, it rolled overboard and was lost forever. Not a native was in sight. All had apparently swum back to the island. To put in an hour or so while the storm was abating, we collected all the canoes and tied them together and sailed them close to the cliff. Then, leaving them there we could see the natives swim out to them and paddle them back to land.

I collected a very nice bunch of paddles and other weapons out of these canoes. We never told anyone of this experience. Jack was afraid he might go to jail for shooting at them. First cleaning up the tacks, I filled the forehold with everything I could get in it from these canoes, selling the collection of beautifully carved paddles for several hundred dollars later in Australia. At any rate, Jack had kept my word with the chief by making lots of noise.

Niuafo'ou is of volcanic formation and has lots of shakes. Every little while when the volcano gets active the natives all beat it to the hills. All their houses have stone foundations. I got from this island some of the best oranges, bananas, pineapples, young coconuts and breadfruit that we had yet eaten on the voyage.

The chief, Folofile, was a nasty old devil and I was not at all sorry to leave this island. Though his island was part of the Tonga group, he told me that he and his people were not of these people. His people were a race of their own. They were not Fijians. They were better men than the Fiji people, and often in the old days would go to Fiji by canoe and beat the Fijians in battle, which of course, always ended in a "long pig" feast. I certainly did not like Folofile.

If this old chief gave me a wrong impression of his people, it was no fault of mine. I so enthused Voss with the chief's blowing that he believed me, and if Voss's cannon shot killed any of these cannibals they could only blame their finish on their egotistical chief.

When I look back at this island now, I think what a poor bunch of sports the whole lot was. This man Flower, born with a white skin, and all he could tell me was that I should have a permit to land at the island. The chief, so filled with his historical forefathers' episodes that he could only think of "long pig" feeding.

Without thinking, I passed all this to Jack, apparently filling him with thoughts of cannibal feeding, so that all he wished to do was to hit the broad Pacific, regardless of weather. This we did on October 15th, shaping a course for Suva, the capital of Fiji, and for three days more we never saw the sun. Yet so accurate was Jack's reckoning that he pulled out of the ocean a real Cleopatra Needle. Here was this huge and high rocky thing, sticking out of the ocean like a cluster of saw teeth, and not a beach or coconut tree near it. It had nothing but the waves to keep it company, and certainly gave me the creeps. I will look up the name of this needle later, but get this, Jack Voss steered for it and found it at three o'clock in the afternoon, after three days without a sight with the sextant. We found it by his dead-reckoning.

It was, I think, that same night, and goodness knows how hard it was blowing, that once more I smelled land. It was so strong that I called Jack out of a sound sleep in the bunk and asked him to heave to. It was the first time I ever saw Jack incautious. He took a look around and said, "Keep her on her course." About two-thirty in the morning I heard the breakers, but do all I could, I could not get away from that graveyard sound. It was of no use to call Jack. The reef was there and the waves were smashing on top of it. I almost crept away, but I think it was that seventh heaven which picked us up, dropped the *Tilikum* fair and square on the centre of her keel and quite on the centre of the reef. Then came the next wave to smash all broad side on the canoe's twenty-eight foot hull and, as a chip in a whirlpool of the Grand Canyon, it was turned upside down and down side up, how many times I do not know.[67] The hatch of the cabin was shut and no water worth speaking of could get in to Jack. When I came to after being pitched out of the cockpit, far enough away not to be ground between the coral and the canoe, I was swimming in the over-wash of the waves pitching over the reef. There was no sign of the canoe, not a sight or a sound could I see or hear of her. I knew I was inside a lagoon, but where it was, or what it was, I had no idea. Only one thing possessed my mind, and that was that like many other lagoons it was full of sharks, and the longer I thought of them the larger they became. My mind was never brighter than right then. Although I was swimming or treading water, my eyes and nose were full of the sea. By striking out into the lagoon I might, with luck, find a shallow place to rest until daybreak, but without luck I might swim all night only to find a resting place in some shark's belly. Hobson[68] had nothing on me, so I decided to stay with the reef, hoping that Jack would find me before I became exhausted. Every wave that broke over the reef shot me into the lagoon, and each time I would swim back to get away from the sharks, only to get another pounding by tons of water. At first I felt the coral skinning my shins, my arms and my elbows. Then a sharp pain would tell me of a toe-nail displaced, but always I would come back. Extra large waves, casting tons of water over the reef, would throw me further into the lagoon. Frantically would I put on more steam to reach the reef away from the sharks, only to get more Hell from the coral. Just how long this fight kept up, I do not know. I think I can remember sunshine coming slowly, and from there I apparently had one idea, and that was to hang on to the coral reef at all cost. How it punished my body showed afterwards.

[67] Voss leaves this wreck out of his book. Luxton could never understand why Voss, who never took a chance, was so indifferent that night.

[68] "Hobson's Choice," a phrase meaning "no choice at all."

Jack told me he found me at ten a.m. and he was quite sure that I was dead. There was a sand beach and some coconut trees handy so he was willing to bury me. I guess his intentions were good. When I came to, I was lying face down in a sandy spot and from the moisture around my face all the sea water had evidently run out of my lungs and innards. Jack was down at the edge of the water, nothing on but a shirt, no boots or pants, and he was examining the hull of the canoe. Right out of the dead past of at least ten hours I could read every move Voss was making. Spitting out another teaspoonful of water and rising to my feet, I teetered towards the canoe. Suddenly Jack caught sight of me, and I am sure that he was scared half to death. The damn fool thought me dead, and it was only because he was more interested in the canoe that he had not buried me first before examining it. I certainly blssed that paper Swan held in Apia. But goodness gracious, what a mess my body was in. I had no toe-nails, no finger-nails, and all the front of my body was as raw as a butcher's hind-leg of beef. My knees were scraped to the bone and my shins also, such was the roughness of my treatment by the coral. Vaseline and sweet oil bandages covered my whole body, yet for days I was too tired to even think of pain. About the third day I realized what coral poisoning was. Every part of my body swelled up to tremendous size. The canoe being almost as complete a wreck as myself, we stayed in this lagoon for several days. Every mast had to be restepped and it was no easy job for one man. Finally, Jack said that the job was finished. I asked him to go ashore and get me as many green coconuts as he could find. This he did, returning an hour or so later with a bushel of very fine nuts. Twice more he made the trip to the coconut groves, each time returning with two dozen nuts. The last time he handed me a skull, the top and frontal bones of which were all gone. Some loving friend had hit him so hard the pieces must have gone through to his boots. Jack said, "There is a pile of these fellows over there under some banana trees that would make a pile of buffalo bones on the prairies look small." I sent him back to look for more skulls but he could find none better than the one he had brought me. I am quite sure that Jack would have gone to Hell and back for me in those few days, so glad was he to see me alive. Indeed, it was one of the few times that he showed any fellow feelings, and in my weak state it helped me to come back.

We discovered afterwards that the reef and lagoon that we blew over and into was called Duff Reef. From there into Suva we passed dozens and dozens of wrecks throughout the islands. What a terribly pitiful sight it was to see the ribs and spines of once beautiful boats rotting away at the constant motion of the ocean and coral.

On October 17th, late at night, we sighted Suva Harbour lights. As this harbour is full of shoal water, and requires a pilot to enter at night, we hove to until morning. With the buoys as guides to deep water, we got well into the bay the next morning. The harbour master, Captain Clark, met us in his launch and took us in tow.

We stayed in Suva for several days and were treated most kindly by everyone. Our boat was a tremendous curiosity. We landed as soon as possible. I got to a hotel and had a doctor brought, who examined me thoroughly. He as much as told me that I would be committing suicide to continue on with the *Tilikum* in the condition I was in. I had never got back anything like my normal weight after the first six thousand miles, and the break against me on Duff Reef seemed to sap the last kick I had left. After thinking it over that night, I got up in the morning with the full intention of finding a suitable man to continue on at once with Voss.

Going into the bar of the hotel, I heard a voice say, "I would not be afraid to sail in her anywhere." I turned to see who was speaking and saw a very fine looking chap, quite clean cut. Half an eye would tell you he was a sailor. He was talking to Jack Voss. I went to them at once and Jack said:

"Norm, the doctor told me yesterday you will have to go to Australia by steamer. Either that or write Swan that you decided to commit suicide."

"Whom," I said, "can you get to take my place?"

"I think I have the man right here, if you are willing. Either our agreement stands, or perhaps you would rather pay him sailor's wages."

Then Jack introduced me to Louis Begent, who was a native of Tasmania, of English descent, perhaps not more than twenty-five years old. A mighty fine chap he appeared to be, and at breakfast that morning and the next day, being pretty much in his company, I got to like him fine. I told Jack I was agreeable to his joining the *Tilikum*.

Most of that day was spent in cleaning out the canoe's holds and lockers of curios I had collected on the trip. Very much against my wishes, Voss loaded these self-same empty spaces with many brands of gin and other liquors. When I objected, he told me in very plain language that it was none of my business this trip, so what could I say or do? I cautioned Begent to be most careful, telling him I had at no time carried booze on board, because when Voss got too much he never knew what he did. Anyway, they cleared for Sydney, Australia, some sixteen or seventeen hundred miles away, booze and all.[69] A kindly captain of a steamer gave me passage to Sydney. I regret very much that I lost, later in my travels, my diary on Suva so what this captain's name was or what his boat was called, I cannot remember. During the entire voyage to Australia I was confined most of the time to my cabin. The Suvian doctor's predictions that I was sick were quite true, but all the stewards and officers on the ship were fine to me. Special foods and services seemed no trouble and many a time from my heart have I thanked them.

It was not until away in November, perhaps about the twentieth, that I began to feel much better and was moving around, although I was quite forty pounds lighter than I should have been. I was sitting under the huge shady trees at Manly. They lined the main street of the

---

[69] "How well I remember it. I did everything I could to get Begent to throw the liquor away. I told him Voss was a devil when full," Luxton wrote elsewhere.

town, which was across the harbour some seven miles from Sydney. I was anxious about the *Tilikum*, which at the very least calculation, was ten days overdue. Two and three times a day I would get messages from the harbour master's office at Sydney telling me there was no sight or word of the *Tilikum*. I had almost made up my mind to give the canoe and crew up for lost when in the afternoon, about two p.m., who should step up on the verandah but Jack Voss himself. I would say I was glad to see him. He told me for an hour of storms I had never dreamed of. In none of our experiences of over ten thousand miles had we ever had anything like it. Then he told me the worst of all. Jack Begent had fallen overboard with the compass and was drowned. A sea had swept the boat when he was changing tack and washed him overboard. Needless to say, I was shocked and grieved at the terrible news.

Jack brought the canoe over to Manly, where we beached her. Putting a wall of canvas all around her, we lectured on our trip across the Pacific, charging a sixpence for admission. While we did good business, there was always something missing in the tone of the crowds who attended.

For a week after I was convalescent I had all the newspapers in Sydney working for the *Tilikum* pending her arrival. When I registered Louis Begent's death at the harbour office every paper dropped us as if the *Tilikum* had never existed. Voss had to go to the hospital. The last thousand miles had been too much for him. But even if the papers acted as if they did not believe Jack Voss's story of Begent's death,[70] everyone was kind to me. The mayor of Manly gave me, free

---

[70] "I feel sure he killed Begent. It was a drunken fight without doubt that finished Begent. In fact he [Voss] refused to say he did not when I accused him of it. Begent was not his first according to his own stories. I might have been one as well, but knowing him as I did, I was always ready for him. Voss landed in Australia days overdue, and was in hospital for weeks from exposure and sickness he contracted through the women on the islands," Luxton wrote elsewhere.

of rent, the use of enough beach to show the *Tilikum* and the sail-maker fixed me up with canvas for the walls of our show house. Later we moved to Newcastle, and then to Melbourne, where Voss and I parted company, never hearing directly from one another again, although to this day I own two-thirds of one half of the *Tilikum*, one-sixth of it being used to pay the wages of the sailor at any time I was away from the boat. Of Jack's trips around the world, entitled *The Venturesome Voyages of Captain Voss*, I can surely recommend it to every one, more particularly to sailing men. Jack Voss, without doubt, had the most wonderful store of sailing knowledge ever in one man's brain of this day and age. There was never a doubt in my mind that Jack was born ages after his time, or else he carried into this life the complete knowledge he acquired in a previous one of Viking lore. Jack Voss was not a foolhardy brave man, neither was he a fool. Cautious—yes—to the furthest extreme. Never did he ever take a chance with wind, waves, weather, or unknown harbours at night.[71] Safety first, always, was his slogan, and because of that very stand he lasted longer than most sailors. The knowledge he accumulated he never forgot and in his book he passes his knowledge on, which is admitted today by the best yachtsmen of the world to be invaluable.

One more page and this short account of the adventures of the crew of the *Tilikum* will close. At the house where I stayed in Manly the landlady was a firm believer in fortune-tellers, spiritualists and so forth. There was hardly a block in parts of Sydney that did not carry many signs of such business. This lady continually kept telling me to go and consult her special "advice-giver." She was infallible, she could not tell me wrong. This was all before Jack Voss's arrival with the *Tilikum* and me about crazy with anxiety. So one morning I took the ferry at Manly for Sydney, and after four hours by street car I found my landlady's spiritualist. On being admitted to the house by a

---

[71] Voss took a chance at Duff Reef, Luxton infers elsewhere.

large woman, who was drying her hands and arms on her apron, and who smelled of soap from the family wash, I asked for Mrs. X. She escorted me into a room furnished with some kitchen chairs and a small wooden table, asking me to be seated and she doing likewise. She told me that she was Mrs. X. I told her I came for a reading. At once and without any hesitation she went into a trance, her eyes wide open all the time, and asked me what I wanted to know.

"Are all my folks at home and well?" I asked. She told me of one person in my father's house, then of another. All through the family she went, person by person, until all were accounted for, even to a white Spitz dog and the black cat. No one in Australia knew my family but myself, so it could not have been any put-up job. She also told me of friends in other parts of America, answering just as accurately. As to the *Tilikum*, she told of storm and trouble and Jack Voss, but of Louis Begent she could not see or tell me. I paid this lady a sovereign and considered it well spent for a half hour's wonderment that Canadian boys were not used to. This lady told me that all the money she received for such "readings," as she called them, she gave to a children's home next door to her own. This I found out to be true.

Some weeks afterwards, when showing the canoe at Manly, this same lady dropped in to see us. It was just closing time and Jack was tying and closing the canvas door. Mrs. X. climbed up into the cockpit of the *Tilikum* and her big husband followed her. Sitting down, she went off into one of her trances. Her husband was not at all concerned, he kept looking into the cabin and sizing up the rigging of the boat. All this time Mrs. X. was talking. In the most minute detail, she described a fight taking place in the cockpit of the *Tilikum*, and so harrowing was it put that my flesh all went goosey. Suddenly, putting her hands to her face, she cried and screamed with huge tears running through her fingers. Still this demonstration had no apparent effect on her spouse, who went on examining rope and tackle and could have, I'll bet, gone home and described everything in the canoe rigging. It was easy to see that he had been a sailor, as most men who live around Sydney harbour are. Finally, with a few half dozen soft pedal sobs, Mrs. X. came out of her trance and, grabbing her husband's arm, almost swept him out of the cockpit, so anxious was she to get away, telling him she was sure it was a bad, wicked place.

I have often wondered at what age of that old war canoe's life Mrs. X. was describing. For without doubt the old canoe during her hundred-odd years of paddling, had seen many a bloody fight around the Island of Vancouver when she was owned by one of the most bloodthirsty races of North America.

When Jack and I separated in Australia it was the last we saw of each other, though through the press and mutual acquaintances I often heard of him for years. After a wonderful and eventful voyage with the *Tilikum* across the Indian Ocean and South Atlantic twice, he finally landed in London, England, and as mentioned in this script, I can recommend his book to all who love adventures. Without the aid of any kind of mechanical power he accomplished what no human being has ever done and possibly will never attempt again. What eventually ever became of him I could never find out. The last I heard of him he was somewhere in the Orient, and those who claimed to know say that one day he sailed away from the island of Japan in a wee small boat, a much smaller boat than he had ever attempted before, over the horizon of the broad Pacific. He disappeared, never to be heard of again. If such is the case he died the death he always looked forward to, and without a doubt met his end in the manner a brave sailor should.

Australian climate proved too warm for me, a snow-born Canadian, so it was not long before I signed on as an A.B.[72] with one of the Canadian Pacific steamships and had a much rougher time reaching Victoria, British Columbia, than the *Tilikum* had reaching Australia.

---

[72] Able-bodied seaman.

Twenty-five years and more have passed since that time. Many things are forgotten, many more things remembered, so that reading this journal once more I see that it would not be hard to enlarge it to twice its length. Perhaps for the reader's sake it is well that it is as short as it is. One more word and I am through. "Would you repeat the trip again?" I am often asked. Quite candidly and truly *NO*, but not for anything would I have missed it. Under different circumstances, with a larger boat, the voyage would have been divine, and in such a boat if Voss were master, I would not have hesitated to go anywhere the winds and storms would drive.

Epilogue

It didn't take Norman Luxton long to recover from his ordeal aboard the *Tilikum*. Shortly after he returned to Canada in 1902, he went to the tiny town of Banff, Alberta, to recover his health. Back then, Banff was known for curing what ailed people through the medicinal qualities of its hot springs. These could be enjoyed through soaking at places like Dr. Brett's Sanitorium and the Cave and Basin or through internal consumption as Lythia Water.

Whether it was due to the magic water or the magnificent scenery and fresh mountain air, Luxton regained his health. He then set out to make Banff famous for its spectacular mountain scenery and wildlife. He took on the Alps, marketing the Canadian Rockies as one better—or even more than one better: "Fifty Switzerlands in One" was his booster-ish message. He started a boat tour operation on the fjord-like Lake Minnewanka and opened the Sign of the Goat curio store, which still stands on the south side of the bridge across the Bow River in the Town of Banff. He opened the Lux Theatre and King Edward Hotel on Banff Avenue, and started the Banff *Crag and Canyon* newspaper, which is still published today. And he developed the particular tendency of Banff businessmen to resent the rules of the national park, which, together with the scenery, are the basis of their prosperity. He became an early proponent of "self-government" for the town of Banff.

Norman also married into the original pioneer family of Alberta's Bow Valley. The McDougalls were missionaries and pioneers long before the Canadian Pacific Railway was a glimmer in John A. Macdonald's bloodshot eye. They had known the great herds of buffalo. George McDougall, the patriarch, froze to death in a blizzard on Calgary's Nose Hill. Georgina, Norman's wife, was the daughter of David McDougall, a son of the Reverend George. She was the first white child born in what is now Alberta. Norman's charming written effort to woo her is contained in Eleanor Luxton's original Introduction.

Luxton also pursued his strong interest in First Nations culture by creating, along with Alberta's first great philanthropist, Eric Harvie, the Luxton Museum of the Plains Indians on the banks of the Bow River in Banff. Norman's flair for the dramatic still can be seen there today in the life-sized re-creation of a Blackfoot sun dance—complete with thongs ripping through the dancer's pectoral muscles—and in the Charlie Biel bronze action diorama of a buffalo jump.

Norman's accounts of collecting artifacts and of photographing a First Nations' burial cave will likely shock the modern sensibilities of many readers. But he was a man of his times. Throughout his life he showed a strong interest in preserving First Nations culture. He worked hard to help the Stoney people through the influenza epidemic of 1918 and was made an honourary chieftain of both the Stoney and Blackfoot people. We do well to remember the historian's admonition not to judge yesterday's people by today's standards.

Norman also had a quirky sense of humour. It can be seen in the back of his curio store—now called Luxton's Trading Post—where the withered and gruesome "Merman of the Great Lakes" is on display in the back room. And Norman still had one big adventure left in him. He conceived and participated in the great buffalo round up that brought Michel Pablo's buffalo herd to Canada—to the outrage of United States' President Theodore Roosevelt, who thought it should remain in Montana.

After the great buffalo round up, Norman settled into his life as one of the leading citizens of Banff, a community that did not lack for interesting people in his day. The editorial page of his *Banff Crag and Canyon* newspaper gave him the opportunity to make known his views on a wide variety of subjects. He continued his interest in collecting First Nation's cultural products, managed the Banff Indian Days for years, judged the Indian Village at the Calgary Stampede, and became fluent in Stoney, a Siouan language. He was a trophy hunter, an upland game bird and duck hunter, and he supported the conservation group Ducks Unlimited. Luxton also used the taxidermy skills he learned in boyhood to serve an international clientele with trophies and furs.

Norman and Georgina had one child, Eleanor, to whom we owe publication of *Tilikum: Luxton's Pacific Crossing*. Norman Luxton died in Calgary in 1962 at the age of 86. He was buried in Banff, a town that in many places still bears his imprint.

—HARVEY LOCKE
Cambridge, Massachusetts
February, 2002